SHAQUILLE O'NEAL

Recent Titles in Greenwood Biographies

SHAQUILLE O'NEAL

A Biography

Murry R. Nelson

GREENWOOD BIOGRAPHIES

GREENWOOD PRESS
WESTPORT, CONN. • LONDON

Library of Congress Cataloging-in-Publication Data

Nelson, Murry R.
    Shaquille O'Neal: a biography / Murry R. Nelson.
        p. cm.— (Greenwood biographies)
    Includes bibliographical references and index.
    ISBN 0–313–33759–4 (alk. paper)
    1. O'Neal, Shaquille.   2. Basketball players—United States—Biography.   I. Title.
    GV884.O54N45   2007
    796.323092—dc22[B]   2006028628

British Library Cataloguing in Publication Data is available.

Library of Congress Catalog Card Number: 2006028628
ISBN: 0–313–33759–4
ISSN: 1540–4900

First published in 2007

Greenwood Press, 88 Post Road West, Westport, CT 06881
An imprint of Greenwood Publishing Group, Inc.
www.greenwood.com

Printed in the United States of America

The paper used in this book complies with the
Permanent Paper Standard issued by the National
Information Standards Organization (Z39.48–1984).

10   9   8   7   6   5   4   3   2   1

CONTENTS

Photo essay follows page 70

SERIES FOREWORD

In response to high school and public library needs, Greenwood developed this distinguished series of full-length biographies specifically for student use. Prepared by field experts and professionals, these engaging biographies are tailored for high school students who need challenging yet accessible biographies. Ideal for secondary school assignments, the length, format and subject areas are designed to meet educators' requirements and students' interests.

Greenwood offers an extensive selection of biographies spanning all curriculum related subject areas including social studies, the sciences, literature and the arts, history and politics, as well as popular culture, covering public figures and famous personalities from all time periods and backgrounds, both historic and contemporary, who have made an impact on American and/or world culture. Greenwood biographies were chosen based on comprehensive feedback from librarians and educators. Consideration was given to both curriculum relevance and inherent interest. The result is an intriguing mix of the well known and the unexpected, the saints and sinners from long-ago history and contemporary pop culture. Readers will find a wide array of subject choices from fascinating crime figures like Al Capone to inspiring pioneers like Margaret Mead, from the greatest minds of our time like Stephen Hawking to the most amazing success stories of our day like J.K. Rowling.

While the emphasis is on fact, not glorification, the books are meant to be fun to read. Each volume provides in-depth information about the subject's life from birth through childhood, the teen years, and adulthood.

A thorough account relates family background and education, traces personal and professional influences, and explores struggles, accomplishments, and contributions. A timeline highlights the most significant life events against a historical perspective. Bibliographies supplement the reference value of each volume.

ACKNOWLEDGMENTS

I didn't really know the details of Shaquille O'Neal's life before writing this book, and I have become a great fan of Shaquille, the player and the person. I have had help in getting this project from research to published book, and I want to recognize some people for their assistance. First, my wonderful staff assistant, Diane Paules, who has read many drafts to improve the text and properly format what I have written. Jacob Edmondson, my trusty representative of the adolescent age group and a ninth grader at State College (PA) Area High School, read drafts of the writing and gave me candid and useful responses. My wife, Elizabeth, an Instructor of English at Penn State, provided feedback and support, as she always does. My editor, Kristi Ward, offered support and insightful suggestions and was always swift in her responses.

Despite this aid, everything that I have written represents my thoughts and ideas. Any mistakes are mine, as are any opinions. As I said, I have grown to greatly appreciate Shaquille O'Neal and hope that this book captures the sense of pleasure and wonder that he has with the world.

INTRODUCTION

In 1989, when Shaquille O'Neal entered the college ranks, playing for LSU, he was seen as a new, "advanced" model of a college basketball center. He not only was tall, but he was wide, strong, and powerful. His impact on the game was immediate and there was some notion that the Shaquille "prototype" would be repeated in other colleges throughout the United States. But there wasn't a lot of success in trying to find Shaquille O'Neal clones; he was simply a one-of-a-kind phenomenon. Instead of duplicating him, teams sought to neutralize him with double and triple teams or with excessive fouling. Finally, the abuse became too much and he left school early to join the professional ranks.

In the National Basketball Association (NBA), similar events occurred. Shaquille was too large for tall, skinny centers to handle and too big for more rugged, shorter players to contain. In addition he had surprisingly quick feet, so it was difficult to defend against him. As in college, there was almost no one quite like Shaquille in the NBA.

In addition Shaquille was highly quotable, often willing to pose for a variety of photos, and made charitable work almost second nature. Still he was seen by many as a big, rough player who played selfishly. Those critics were seemingly justified as Shaquille won NBA scoring and rebounding awards, but never an NBA championship. Over a period of years, that view changed as Shaquille's teams became consistent winners, finally securing an NBA title in 2000. His winning ways and his continued charitable deeds made him more and more popular, and by 2004, when he was traded to the Miami Heat, many viewed him as one of the most likable people in the NBA.

Through the years Shaquille also made rap music CDs and a number of films; and he was prominent in commercials for Taco Bell, Pepsi, Radio Shack, and the Icy Hot patch, among many others. He is the highest paid player in the NBA and he has invested in diverse companies and projects. As he winds down his career, he could be content in retirement. Instead he continues to seek new projects, including a possible career in law enforcement.

Dozens of short biographies have been written on Shaquille O'Neal and he has co-authored two autobiographies. I have drawn on many of these books, as well as many newspaper and magazine accounts of his exploits. In many ways Shaquille is bigger than life, and he is one of the few athletes who is immediately recognizable on sight or just by the mention of his first name. This book examines Shaquille's life and many of the social events that have helped to shape his life and his world.

TIME LINE: SIGNIFICANT EVENTS IN THE LIFE OF SHAQUILLE O'NEAL

March 6, 1972	Born in Newark, New Jersey.
1974	Lucille O'Neal and Phil Harrison marry.
1981	Family moves to Fort Stewart, Georgia.
1983	Family moves to Germany and American Army base.
1987	Family moves back to the United States to San Antonio, Texas.
1989	Shaq leads his Cole High School team to Texas AAA Championship.
Fall 1989	Shaquille enrolls at Louisiana State University.
March 1991	Shaquille is named Southeastern Conference Player of the Year.
May 1991	Shaquille named College Player of the Year by the Associated Press, United Press International, and Sports *Illustrated*.
March 1992	Shaquille repeats as Southeastern Conference Player of the Year.
April 1992	Shaquille announces that he will forgo senior year and declares his intention to be in the NBA draft.
June 24, 1992	Shaquille selected as Number 1 pick in NBA draft by the Orlando Magic.
February 1993	Rookie Shaquille is voted a starting berth in the NBA All-Star game.

May 1993	Shaquille is named Rookie of the Year in the NBA.
Summer 1993	Shaquille has first film role in *Blue Chips*.
November 1993	Shaquille's album, "Shaq Diesel" debuts on Billboard chart at Number 11.
April 1994	The Magic make NBA playoffs for first time in franchise history, but lose in first round.
August 1994	Shaquille is named most valuable player in World Championship of Basketball held in Ontario, Canada.
October 1994	Shaquille is named USA Basketball Male Athlete of the Year.
April 1995	Shaquille wins the NBA scoring title with an average of 29.3 points per game.
June 1995	Shaq leads the Magic to the Eastern Conference Championship, but they lose in the NBA finals to the Houston Rockets.
April 1996	Shaq's grandmother, Odessa Chamblis, who helped raise him, dies.
April 1996	Shaq and the Magic win the Atlantic Division title.
July 1996	Shaq signs $121 million seven-year contract with the Los Angeles Lakers.
July-August 1996	Shaquille and his U.S. Olympic teammates on "Dream Team" II win the Olympic Basketball Gold Medal title.
February 2000	Shaq is named Co-MVP of NBA All-Star game.
March 6, 2000	Shaq scores a career-high 61 points on his 28th birthday.
April 24, 2000	Shaq is named MVP for the 1999–2000 season with 120 of 121 votes cast.
June 19, 2000	L. A. Lakers win NBA championship and Shaq is named MVP for the NBA finals.
December 15, 2000	Shaq receives his B.S. in Business from LSU.
April 2001	Shaq's autobiography, *Shaq Talks Back*, is published.
June 2001	The Lakers repeat as NBA champions and Shaq repeats as NBA finals MVP.
June 2002	The Lakers and Shaq win their third NBA title in a row, and Shaq is named finals MVP for the third straight year.

December 26,2002	Shaquille and Shaunie Nelson, mother of two of Shaq's children, marry in Los Angeles.
July 2004	Shaq is traded to the Miami Heat.
April 2005	Miami, led by Shaq and Dwayne Wade, win Southeast Division title, but lose in Eastern Conference Finals.
April 2006	Miami repeats as Southeast Division champions.
June 2006	Miami wins NBA championship.

Chapter 1

FROM NEWARK TO GERMANY: SHAQ'S EARLY YEARS

March 6, 1972 was a cold, dreary day in Newark, New Jersey, with temperatures in the mid-30s and a light wind from the northwest, making spring seem far away. The city was struggling with a transportation strike of subway and bus workers that affected more than 300,000 riders daily, and the announcement of the closing of the Ballantine Brewery in Newark meant thousands of long-time employees would be losing their jobs. The country was still mired in the war in Vietnam. For more than 20 years, the United States had had a role in propping up the government of South Vietnam in the Vietnamese civil war, but President Nixon would finally agree to end American involvement in the war and pull all American troops from that country as part of the peace accord signed in 1973. More than 47,000 American troops had been killed in action.

For 18-year-old Lucille O'Neal the day was strenuous but joyous as she gave birth to her first child, whom she named Shaquille Rashuan O'Neal, after reading the names in a book of Islamic names. Despite his future size, Shaquille was not especially large at birth, weighing in at 7 pounds, 11 ounces. Although Lucille was not Muslim, she was interested in the religion because of the large number of recent Muslim converts in her neighborhood. Five years earlier, when Newark had been torn by race riots, the Muslim community with many African American adherents had helped to calm tension through a positive emphasis on neighborhood and ethnic pride, as well as self-reliance. This made the Muslims admired by many, even if they did not wish to practice the faith. The names, "Shaquille" and "Rashuan" intrigued Lucille because they translated as "little warrior," and she saw her first-born child as needing that strength to overcome a lot of difficulties that Lucille had already endured. Lucille was not married to the baby's father who was a man that she had dated for four years in high school named Joe Toney. Toney had been a basketball star in their Newark high school and had been offered a basketball scholarship to Seton Hall University in nearby South Orange, New Jersey. The Seton Hall Pirates, coached by Bill Raftery (later an ESPN college basketball announcer), were not yet a Big East power, and Toney did not seem to apply himself to either his basketball or his academic work and left the university. It was this same lack of commitment that Lucille O'Neal recognized and she, thus, gave her child her last name, rather than that of the father, with whom she had already parted ways.

Shortly after finishing high school, Lucille gave birth and went on welfare. This was not an uncommon pattern in Newark in the early 1970s, particularly among African American women. Of the 124,000 births to African American women, ages 15 to 24 in Newark listed in the 1970 Census, 32,000 were to single mothers. For those between 15 and 19 years old, almost 90 percent of the 16,500 births were to single mothers. So Lucille O'Neal was fairly typical of her counterparts in giving birth while single and going directly onto welfare; there, however, the similarities ended. Lucille was determined to go to work, support her son, and help him to overcome the poverty and disappointment that characterized the life of many African Americans in Newark.

Lucille envisioned her son going to college and becoming successful, but the odds against that were long. At that time the median number of school years completed by African American males in Newark was 10. That meant that half of the African American males in that city had completed 10th grade, but half had not. Only 32 percent of African American males actually graduated from high school, and the percentage was decidedly lower among the poorest of them. Lucille was determined that she and her son would beat those percentages, that her "little warrior" would be a high school graduate and go on to college, but she knew that she had to get off welfare first.

Welfare in the United States originally came about during the Great Depression of the 1930s. With so many people out of work, President Franklin Roosevelt proposed a system to aid unemployed people until they could return to work. The notion was, and always has been, that welfare would be a short-term solution that people would use, often because of a sudden catastrophic illness or job loss. Unfortunately, many people in the 1960s to 1990s fell into what was referred to as "the welfare trap." Children grew up in families where the family was on welfare on a long-term basis because there were no employed workers. The children emulated that same pattern and the number of welfare recipients continued to grow. Lucille O'Neal resolved that that would not happen in her case.

LUCILLE'S FAMILY

Lucille's family was originally from Dublin, Georgia, which is about midway between Macon and Statesboro. In 1904, a pair of African American men were convicted of killing a local Statesboro white couple, but before the convicted killers could be removed from the courtroom, a large crowd of whites burst in, took the defendants out, and lynched them. Then a mob of whites swept through the local African American community, lynching and beating a number of innocent black residents and convincing many African Americans to move out of the region. Although Lucille's great-grandparents were not directly affected by this event, they did learn that black folks would be wise to associate as little as possible with white people in the South.

Until the Depression, the vast majority of African Americans in the United States lived in the South. Most were the direct descendants of the slaves brought to the United States from Africa to work on plantations, and the blacks in most Southern states far outnumbered the whites by the time of the Civil War. After the war ended in 1865, the period of Southern Reconstruction saw African Americans achieving political strength and economic gains for the first time. But in 1877, federal troops that had protected the rights of blacks were withdrawn by President Hayes, as part of a political deal made to ensure his presidency in the disputed election of 1876. Most blacks were reduced to subsistence farming, and that was the situation for Shaquille O'Neal's relatives during the first part of the twentieth century. This way of life continued for African Americans until the Depression, when crop failures and continued economic hardships drove many African Americans to seek new, higher paying jobs in the industrial plants of the cities of the North. This is often referred to as the Great Migration, and it was one of the greatest shifts in population in recent American history.

Lucille's grandparents, Cillar and Hilton O'Neal, were married in 1930 when Cillar was only 15 years old. Her father was also a farmer; he committed suicide shortly before she married, which Shaquille attributed in 2001 to a dispute over another woman. Cillar and Hilton farmed for many years in Georgia but then made their way north to New Jersey. Hilton died in 1965 when Cillar was 50 and she never remarried, instead working and helping her three children raise their families. Hilton and Cillar had two girls, Reba Mae and Ruby Lee, and a boy, Sirlester. Sirlester married Odessa Chambliss in New Jersey and Lucille, their daughter, was born in

1953. The O'Neals are a strong, proud family, which was characteristic of many African American families in the South in the late nineteenth and early twentieth centuries. With little opportunity for economic or political advancement, the black family became a revered structure, which was maintained even as family members moved north. It was ironic that in the 1960s, the social conditions had changed to such a degree that in 1965 a study of black families sounded an alarm that they were failing,[1] and 40 years later the fractured black family is still a major concern for sociologists, policymakers, and leaders in both black and white communities.

Because Shaquille's biological father never participated in Shaquille's life, it serves no purpose to pursue those ancestors. Shaquille was raised by his mother, and, later, her husband, who Shaquille recognizes as his father in every aspect but genetically.

RAISING SHAQ

Lucille O'Neal found raising her little Shaq quite a challenge. After a few months on welfare, Lucille found a job doing clerical work at a youth agency in Newark. She was an intelligent woman who was well organized and responsible. After some months at the youth agency, she took a job at City Hall working in a clerical position in the Payroll Department for the City of Newark. She was still living at home with her grandmother, Cillar (whom she and Shaquille called Muma) O'Neal, and Shaq was either in day care or with his great-grandmother during the day. From early on, Lucille noted that Shaq was a little imp—mischievous, curious, and energetic. He was a real handful, but always loved. His mother recalls that, "At first, Shaquille was hard to manage because he was spoiled rotten. We gave him everything he wanted."[2]

One day Lucille was outside of City Hall when a clean-cut young man got her attention and began chatting with her. Lucille and the young man, Phil Harrison, began seeing each other, first as acquaintances, then as good friends until they fell in love and decided to marry. From the beginning, Phil recognized that it was a "package deal," not just Lucille, and he gave his love to Shaquille as soon as he and Lucille became close. Shaquille was two years old and he didn't immediately take to sharing his mother with someone else, so it took a while for Phil to win over little Shaq, but eventually he did.

PHILIP HARRISON

Philip Harrison's father had come to Newark from Jamaica. He had very strict ideas about raising children, based on his own cultural background in the West Indies. Demographers, people who study populations and population trends, have noted that blacks from the West Indies who immigrate to the United States have a higher rate of success in this country in terms of years of schooling and economic income. There also is greater stability in the families of West Indian immigrants than native African Americans, most notably in the higher percentage of households with fathers present. These factors complement each other. A father in the house means there is a greater likelihood of higher wages, and thus economic security. In addition there is greater likelihood of completing high school and going to college, and one of the most significant factors in increasing one's income as an adult is years of schooling completed. This does not mean that simply coming from the West Indies to the United States will ensure success for an individual, but it does increase the possibility of success.

Philip Harrison had been brought up to appreciate the value of hard work, but, in his own words, he sought to "cut corners" and for a time was a "gangster." Harrison had been a good enough student to go to college and had the support of his family, but in college he spent more time playing cards, chasing girls, and acting crazy, according to him. He attended St. Augustine's College in Raleigh, North Carolina, as well as Essex County College in Newark, but he never graduated. After leaving school he worked at a series of low-paying jobs such as driving a truck, shining shoes, and selling hats. When he met Lucille O'Neal, he was 26 years old and seeking a job working for the city in Newark. Sometimes he held two or three jobs at a time. These were still not enough for him to see a way to achieve real financial security, so shortly after Lucille and Phil were married in 1974, he enlisted in the U.S. Army. He knew that he and his family would have health benefits, he would have job security, and he could be as successful in advancing as he wished to be if he worked hard at his job. From as long as Shaquille can remember, his father worked regularly and instilled in Shaquille an appreciation for hard work and a job well done.

When Phil made his decision to enter the military, it meant that he would be away at basic training for a time, but upon his return he and Lucille set about making a home for the three of them with both Muma, Lucille's grandmother, and Odessa Chamblis, Lucille's mother often either living with them or directly involved with Shaq's childrearing. This led to some disagreements because Shaq had a quality early on that charmed his grandmother and great-grandmother, even when he was being an imp. He was, remember, spoiled, as his mother noted earlier. Phil had been raised with corporal punishment as a way of life by his own father, and he found that approach most appropriate. Shaq recalls being told of an incident that occurred when he was three years old. Muma was in the habit of sneaking a bottle to him at bedtime. Phil felt that this was not a way to harden his son and he took the bottle away, only to have Muma hit him in the head and tell him to "leave that boy alone." So childrearing practices were often inconsistent, and Shaq was quick to learn how to play his various caregivers off one another to get what he wanted. There was no question, however, that Phil used corporal punishment for Shaq's many transgressions, some of which were serious. These included pulling a fire alarm on a dare (and being swiftly apprehended on the military base where it occurred), goofing off in class, petty theft, not being home by a designated time, and getting poor grades. Shaq claimed and Phil agrees that Shaq was paddled often as a child.

Phil was stationed in New Jersey and he and his family lived off base. Their first real home was in Bayonne, New Jersey, about five miles east of Newark across Newark Bay. Shaq recalled that this was when and where Phil first began really disciplining him (without the interference of Muma or Grandma Odessa). Phil was working more than one job and he was not about to let Shaq run wild, so when he was home he made sure that Shaq obeyed his parents, and Phil instilled the rudiments of discipline in the boy. It took a while, however, for those lessons to really set in.

SHAQ'S INTRODUCTION TO SPORTS

Starting at that house in Bayonne, Phil also began teaching his little boy the joys and skills of baseball, football, and basketball. Phil was 6'5" and he had been a good athlete in high school. He knew the games, both physically and mentally, and he both encouraged and demanded hard work and attention from Shaquille. One time he threw a football and told Shaq to let it hit him. After it bounced off Shaq's face and the sting went away, Phil told him that was the worst thing that could happen when the ball headed his way, and that made Shaq feel more confident catching the ball. Shaq developed confidence and good hands, which served him well in all sports. There was a problem, however, in many of these early sports endeavors—Shaq's size.

Even though Shaq had been an average size baby, his ancestry of tall men in the family made his exceptional growth merely a matter of time. By the time he was four, he was the size of an eight-year-old. Lucille used to ride on the train to get to work in Newark, and Shaq often accompanied her and went to day care in Newark. Lucille was constantly questioned by the train conductors, because they did not believe that Shaq was under five, the age for a half-price ticket. Finally, she had to carry his birth certificate with her to satisfy the conductors. This was just the beginning of many people questioning his age. Another challenge for Lucille was finding clothes for Shaq. He was so much bigger than other children his age. He also grew so quickly that many of his clothes did not fit him for long.

By age five, Shaq and his family had moved, once again, this time to Jersey City, New Jersey, where they lived in their first house and his grandmother, Odessa, was a nurse. They later lived in Eatontown, New Jersey, 35 miles south of Newark because Phil was stationed in Eatontown. Shaquille remembers living all over Newark and staying at various relatives' houses throughout northern New Jersey. These early years were tough economic times for the family, but Shaq remembers feeling loved by so many relatives and never being hungry, despite being poor. He grew to love chicken, macaroni, and sandwich meat and he still enjoys those simple foods, even today. Of course his tastes have expanded, but those foods are still favorites and always remind him of growing up in Newark.

In Newark Shaq was mostly around African Americans, but in Bayonne, he was in school with white, Indian, and Puerto Rican kids and he saw, and began to appreciate, ethnic diversity. He never saw one group as good or bad, but was raised, he noted, to judge people individually, not on their ethnic or racial background.

When Shaq was nine he played football more than any other sport. His family had moved to Fort Stewart, Georgia, when Shaq was in fifth grade and football is the most popular team sport in the South. Shaq loved the game and, for a new kid in school, being good at football meant he'd be more popular and have more friends. He played in a league at the fort that allowed children up to 11 –years old to compete, but Shaq was the biggest player in the league and was, again, often questioned about his age. Many teams demanded proof that he was under 12 and were quite surprised to find that he was just 9 years old. Indeed, having skipped first grade, Shaq might have stood out even more if he been on a typical track through school. In the punt, pass, and kick contest, held at the fort, Shaq was the best in his age group of 9- to 10-year-olds. Shaq was big and strong, but he was still awkward because he had grown so quickly, and his coordination had not yet caught up to his size. Playing as a lineman in football, he could easily overcome his awkwardness because of his strength and large "wingspan" of his arms.

Shaq's fifth grade physical education teacher found Shaq easy to coach but at times in need of disciplining. One day, Shaq's conduct was particularly nettlesome and the teacher paddled Shaq. Not long afterwards, Phil Harrison sought out the teacher and confronted him about the paddling.

When the teacher admitted to paddling Shaq, Phil said that he wanted to shake the teacher's hand for properly disciplining his son, as many others had failed to do. As mentioned before, Shaq was quite charming and the combination of that and his size probably deterred most teachers and coaches from considering corporal punishment, but it was a way of life in the Harrison household.

Living in the South was a revelation for Shaq. Despite the Civil Rights movement of the 1960s and various civil rights laws, there were still many instances where whites and blacks did not interact in social situations. This was new for Shaq, a real contrast to both his life in Newark and in Eatontown, New Jersey. But life in Georgia was short-lived, as Phil was posted to Germany and the family prepared to live overseas for the first time when Shaq was 11 or 12 years old.

LIFE IN GERMANY

The American military presence in Germany began right after World War II. After the war, the victorious Allied forces of France, Great Britain, the Soviet Union, and the United States divided responsibility over the defeated Germany. The country was divided into four regions, with each Allied nation having control over that region. The city of Berlin was also similarly divided. The goal was to move Germany toward forming a new democratic government as swiftly as possible. By 1946, the Soviets had indicated their intentions not to cooperate with the other three nations in the goal of total German reunification and began pursuing the creation of a German "puppet" government under the actual control of the Soviet Union. The three Allied nations pursued the creation of what became the Democratic Republic of Germany (West Germany). During this time Germany needed to have some sort of police protection, and the first American military troops acted in that function.

After the German constitution was created in 1948, the Germans took over the police functions that the Allies had taken on, but thousands of Allied troops remained in military bases throughout Germany for security reasons as the era of the Cold War began. This policy continued into the late 1980s. At one point more than 400,000 U.S. troops were stationed in Germany. It had stabilized at about 250,000 by the time Phil Harrison was assigned to Weisbaden, Germany in 1984. Three months later the family was posted to Wildflecken Army Base.

Wildflecken is located in the Fulda Gap region of the state of Bavaria in West Germany, on the border between what was then East and West Germany and close to what was then Czechoslovakia. The army base functioned as a major training area for American troops in Europe. Phil Harrison was an army supply sergeant and a drill instructor, and he was integral in the training of troops. He applied that training to raising Shaquille.

By the time Shaq and his parents moved to Germany, there were three other children in the family. When Shaq was about six, his sister, Lateefah, was born and she was followed in swift succession by sister Ayesha and his brother, Jamal, who is eight years younger than Shaq. Being the big brother brought a lot of responsibility to Shaq, and he became very close to his siblings. At the same time he also continued to get into trouble for various petty offenses. He stole items, mostly by shoplifting. He also hung out with a number of kids who either used or had access to drugs and alcohol. Shaq used neither because he was not interested but primarily because he knew his father would give him the whipping of his life if he ever used any of those substances. Still he was often defiant, and he remembers that he was beaten by his father, almost every day. Shaq says today that it was deserved, but at that time, he greatly resented his father and continued to act out.

Moving as often as they did and being poorer than a lot of kids, Shaq had to endure teasing on a regular basis. Sometimes it was because he was so big. Kids would call him Sasquatch, Shaqueer, and Shaquilla the Gorilla. He also was teased because his clothes were not always as nice as those of his peers. He wore the same clothes more often and had fewer toys and sports equipment than did other military kids, especially the officers' kids, of whom he was very envious. He was angry a lot, but he tried to act cool. That didn't last long, however, and he became a bully and a thief. Kids would tease him and he'd respond by smashing their faces into a desk or punching them. That behavior diminished after he beat up a Georgia classmate who had identified him as the person who threw something in class. After school he found the boy, knocked him around, and kicked him when he fell to the ground. At that point the boy began having an epileptic seizure and Shaq was paralyzed with fear. Fortunately, someone was nearby who knew what was happening and took proper care of the young man, but the incident made Shaq see that he could really hurt someone if he wasn't more careful. He stopped the bullying behavior, but aspects of it returned when the family moved to Germany, which angered Shaq greatly.

The move to Germany was great for Phil's career, but awful for Shaq, and he begged to be sent back to the United States to live with relatives in Newark. His parents refused to consider this request, so he acted out more and more to try to force them to let him go back. He broke into cars, threatened kids, did poorly in school, and was a big problem for his parents. His father knew what he was trying to do, but told him that he wasn't sending Shaq back to Newark. He said that Shaq had better start listening to him or he would beat Shaq's butt every single day. And, according to Shaq, he got those beatings, as it took quite a while for him to stop being a "punk." He was still breaking into cars, stealing things, beating people up, and talking back to teachers. Eventually he got scared out of this behavior because of his father and because of the criminal activity that the kids he hung with decided to try.

Shaq hung with older kids in a gang called the Furious Five. Besides theft and intimidation, they also got into break dance wars, and Shaq became a good break dancer, despite his size and awkwardness. He was 6'6" by the time he was 13 years old. One day his gang friends decided to break into a car on the army base in order to steal some sunglasses they saw on the dashboard. And while they were at it, they figured they might as well steal the car, too. Shaq decided that this was not for him and said so. His gang called him a punk and he just said, yes, I am, and walked away. The kids were quickly caught and punished for the acts. Shaq figured that if he had been a part of that affair, he would have likely served some time in a juvenile detention facility and would have gotten the beating of his life from his father.

There were times that Shaq had behavioral "relapses," but his parents became more aware of these episodes. One time he came to breakfast wearing neat clothes and being overly polite to his parents. Naturally, they were a bit suspicious and Phil discreetly followed Shaquille to school. There he saw Shaq unbutton his shirt, roll up his sleeves, and clamor about the classroom. According to Phil, when Shaquille saw him, he froze and Phil told him to go back and sit down. He wanted Shaquille to know that his dad might be there when he didn't expect him to be. Shaq's behavior continued to improve.

The army base was boring to Shaq and he wanted to make some money as a young teen, so he took a job at McDonald's on the base. His most despised job was fry detail, which involved mopping up all the drippings left in the fryer after it was used. That was too much for him and he quit almost immediately. His new job was baby sitter for his three young siblings every summer day while his parents worked. He handled every aspect of child care, making meals, changing diapers, taking them to the park, reading stories, supervising nap time, washing dishes, and whatever else was needed. As his sister recalled, he also made them laugh a lot. Shaq had always been kind of a clown in school, and at home and he loved the attention he received from making people laugh. After the summer was over, there were many days when Shaq continued to be responsible for child care. Shaq's parents liked to sleep in some days, and it was Shaq who entertained and cared for his younger siblings, who by this time were seven, six, and five. In Shaq's 2001 autobiography, his sister, Ayesha, describes some of their activities. Many were silly games that Shaq would make up and the kids loved. For example, Shaq would make their Cabbage Patch dolls break dance. He also taught his siblings how to swim and play basketball. He was, and still is, a good and loyal brother.

NOTES

1. The study was *The Negro Family: The Case for National Action* and was by Daniel P. Moynihan, later a U.S. Senator from New York, as well as the U.S. Ambassador to the United Nations.

2. Shaquille O'Neal, *Shaq Talks Back* (New York: St. Martin's Press, 2001), 11.

Chapter 2

DISCOVERING BASKETBALL

When Shaq was about seven years old, his father began playing basketball with him. Phil had been a good player and was about 6'5", so basketball was special to him, and he wanted Shaquille to learn the game the right way. Phil focused on basketball fundamentals, understanding the game and working hard at improvement. Shaquille was guided by those principles throughout his early years as he learned to play. His growth spurts had made him clumsy, as noted earlier, but Phil helped him to master better footwork, a key to basketball success. Phil worked with Shaquille on proper shooting technique and ball handling.

When Shaquille was about eight, he remembers Phil taking him to see the New York Knicks play in Madison Square Garden. The Knicks were led by Micheal Ray Richardson and Bill Cartwright, with the Hall of Famer Earl Monroe, finishing out his career. The Knicks were not a good team, but they were all-stars in little Shaq's eyes. He treasured that event and it made him think that maybe, one day, he, too, might play in the "Garden." Of course, these are the dreams of so many youngsters when they attend a professional game, but the odds against that actually happening are astronomical. Shaq, of course, didn't know that, but it wouldn't have mattered at that time if he did. He enjoyed the game and it was something that he could share with Phil, so he was interested in getting better at basketball.

One of Phil's on-base jobs in New Jersey gave him access to the base gym and equipment, and he brought home a scuffed-up basketball for Shaquille one day. This was a treasure to Shaq and he kept his ball with him wherever he went. Ayesha Harrison, Shaq's sister, remembers that

Shaq even slept with the ball, sometimes using it as a pillow. Shaq didn't become a basketball star just because he was big. From his youngest years he worked hard at basketball to please Phil and himself. The move to Germany was one of the best things that happened to Shaq for his basketball development. It wasn't that basketball was big in Germany, because it wasn't. Rather it was because there was such a lack of things to do on the base that Shaq spent hours at the gym playing with his friends or by himself.

One of those friends was a boy named Mitch Riles, and he and Shaq played nearly every day. They would play with other kids, but often it was just the two of them. Mitch was Shaq's first close white friend. He also looked, according to Shaq, like Larry Bird, the Boston Celtics star at the time. When they played, Mitch was Bird and Shaq was Magic Johnson, the Lakers' star. To complete the imaginary NBA contests, Riles wore green and white Converse sneakers like the Celtics did, and Shaq wore the gold and purple Converse of the Lakers. They battled every day, often in one-on-one games. It was here that Shaq began to develop his game through repetition and competition. He was getting better, but he was still clumsy at times. At 13 and 6'6", he tried out for the base high school team as a freshman but was cut. That same year a college coach named Dale Brown paid a visit to the Wildflecken Army Base to do a basketball clinic for the soldiers and Shaquille attended.

Dale Brown was an unusual man in many ways. Raised very poor in North Dakota, Brown, a conservative, religious man, decided to try to help others less fortunate than he. He had managed to become wealthy and successful as a basketball coach, so he tried to "give something back" by doing clinics overseas, often at his own expense. And it was on one of those tours that Brown, the coach of Louisiana State University, came to Wildflecken. The clinic involved various drills and information that he shared with the attendees. Because Shaquille was so interested in basketball and the clinic was in the gym, where he spent a lot of time, he attended. His father had encouraged Shaquille to become more knowledgeable about the game, as well as to practice hard at the techniques of the game, so Shaq was glad to be there.

After the clinic ended and Coach Brown was giving autographs to those soldiers who lingered, Shaq asked if he could get some weight-lifting gear to help him strengthen his legs. He explained that, despite his height (Shaq figured that he was about 6'8" then), he was cut from the team and he wasn't strong enough to dunk. Coach Brown listened to Shaquille's laments, then asked him how long he had been in the army. Shaquille shocked Brown by saying that he wasn't in the army and, in fact, was just 13 years old. At that, Brown asked to meet Shaquille's father, who was finally found taking a sauna. While fully dressed, Dale Brown chatted with Phil in the sauna about scholarships to college, but Phil said that a basketball scholarship could wait. First, Shaq needed to prove that he was seriously interested in a college education, which Coach Brown found to be a respectable response, one that he actually agreed with. He then said that he would be watching Shaquille's development closely, as closely as one could when the subject of scrutiny was on an army base in Germany.

That fall (of 1986) Shaquille, now a sophomore, went out for the team at Fulda High School. His coach, then, remembered him as being tall, gawky, determined, and confident.[1] Shaquille was brimming with confidence, in fact, and said that he was going to be the starting center on the team. Despite the coach's skepticism, he put Shaquille on the team and he was, indeed, the starting center in the opening game for the high school team as a 14-year-old sophomore. According to his coach, Ford McMurtry, Shaq scored 16 points in that first game, took down more than 10 rebounds, and outplayed opponents two to three years older than he. He rarely dunked, both because his legs were so skinny and weak and because of the osteitis that he had developed as a result of his break dancing.

Osteitis, or inflammation of the bones, can occur almost anywhere in the body. Shaquille's osteitis was caused by landing hard on his knees while break dancing and was exacerbated by his rapid growth, which resulted in stretching of the bone and an inflamed knee, the swelling of which would lessen as the liquid formed in the knee gradually dissipated. Dancing, however, helped Shaquille become less awkward and to maintain his confidence on the court.

Coach McMurtry of Fulda High was still in his twenties after graduating from Auburn University in Alabama. There he had been a punter on the football team and learned to coach various sports. He had never had an athlete, however, quite like Shaquille O'Neal. The coach was impressed with Shaquille's work ethic and his humility. He never asked for favors or special treatment, although it was obvious to McMurtry that O'Neal was going to be a special player. Some of the moves that he demonstrated in games were still amazing to McMurtry, as he recalled them nearly 10 years later.[2]

Shaquille averaged around 18 points and 12 rebounds per game, and his team revolved around him. By the end of the year, the team was playing well in the small schools league that it was in. (Fulda only had about 250 students). The team won five of its last six games and was headed to a post-season tournament when the Army told Phil that he was being transferred back to the States after nearly three years abroad. When the soldiers in the Fulda community heard that Shaquille and his family were scheduled to depart, they raised nearly $2,000 for him to catch a later flight after the tournament. It seemed to be a good solution for the team and Shaquille, who had grown close to his teammates and coach, but then McMurtry received a call from Lucille. She explained how much she and her husband appreciated the outpouring of community support for Shaquille and how much he loved his teammates and coach, but she was not about to let her "little boy" (he was 6'8", but still just 15 years old) travel alone across the Atlantic, and she wasn't going to leave Germany without him.

So Shaquille played one more victorious game, and after the game Phil burst into the locker room, seeking his son, saying that they had to leave. The coach explained that it would be just a few minutes, but Phil emphasized that they were leaving *now*. With that, McMurtry found Shaq crying in the bathroom, where the two embraced and Shaq thanked his coach for all his support. And then he was gone.

BACK TO THE UNITED STATES AND
HIGH SCHOOL FAME

Sergeant Phil Harrison had been transferred to Brooke Army Medical Center located in Fort Sam Houston in San Antonio, Texas. The fort had been in operation in one form or another since 1845, and the Medical Training Center had been established as the Army's chief medical training center immediately after World War II. More than 20,000 military and civilian personnel worked at the base. Robert G. Cole Junior-Senior High School, named after a Congressional Medal of Honor recipient, was located on the base as part of the Fort Sam Houston Independent School District. This was the school to which Shaquille transferred. It was a small school of about 400 students, but it had established itself as an athletic power in Class 3A of Texas high schools (there are six classes and the smaller schools are in the lower classes) as a Class 3A school in the middle of San Antonio. Because the school was composed of children of military personnel, there was a high transfer rate, both in and out of the district. In previous years the high school had received students who had been all-Germany or all-European, but almost all had failed to live up to this kind of hype because the competition was so much better in the United States.

In the 1970s and 1980s, basketball was still a sport in "development" in Europe. Despite being disappointed before, there were great hopes when the staff encountered Shaquille O'Neal. The season had just ended in Texas, so Shaq did not play any interscholastic basketball in Texas in his sophomore year. He did impress the coaching staff just by his 6'9" frame and enormous feet. He was wearing size 17 shoes and by senior year he was up to a size 20. He was also able to watch NBA play regularly on television now, because regular NBA games were carried on the air through the playoffs in late May. Shaq was able to create his own new moves after watching the NBA players. He also now had the strength to dunk on a regular basis.

Phil had some videotapes of some of Shaq's games in Germany, which he shared with the Cole High School athletic staff, who were duly impressed. Nevertheless, until they actually saw him in action against challenging competition, they were cautiously optimistic. The high school coach wanted Shaq to play in a summer league in order for the coaches and Shaq to get a real feel for his abilities, and Shaq agreed. Initially put in a medium level league, he was swiftly moved up to the top level where he made the all-star team at the end of the summer. His dunks often left everyone in the gym speechless. His coaches remember him as being a hard, cooperative worker who showed up early and left late. He was always asking for suggestions on improving his play, then worked on those things that were suggested. He was the type of player who coaches love—talented, hard-working, and not cocky. He had learned the right lessons from Phil, and the various coaches with whom he had contact in the summer league were universally impressed with Shaquille as a player and as a young man. That spring Shaquille dated his first girlfriend, a track athlete at Cole, but they lived on opposite sides of the enormous army base and saw each other only at school. With summer break, the romance ended.

When school resumed in the fall, Shaq was already well known in the small, close-knit community. His parents joined the Cougar Club, a parent booster club, and his dad often worked on the sidelines, handling the yardage markers for the Cougar football team. Shaquille was a good student, according to his teachers, but all agreed that he still loved to clown. His break dancing days were over, but he could still dress in an attention-getting way and he still loved practical jokes. He also could keep his face "dead pan" while making some outrageous statements, which either brought laughter or confusion to his audience. Shaq was a noted figure in his little high school, and there was great anticipation about how good the Cole High team would be with the addition of this talented giant.

The 1987–1988 Cole High School basketball season was as good as had been hoped. The team, led by Shaq, went undefeated into the state tournament. The team was not only good but the players enjoyed each other immensely, and much of that was due to Shaq and his clowning. The team bus was almost never quiet, with Shaq leading the singing and his teammates beating rhythms. It helped that the team didn't lose, of course, in keeping the atmosphere so free and easy. Even when one of their opponents lost to the visiting Cole squad, Shaq's presence in the gym was exciting. School personnel would often ask the referees to stay in their locker room so that the local fans could be entertained by Shaq's dunking in warm-ups. This was against the rules in Texas high schools and would have resulted in a team technical foul, but with no referees, there was no one to call such a violation, thus the request by the school officials.

In the state tournament, Cole was undefeated before losing to Liberty Hill High School in the regional finals. Shaquille blamed himself for the loss when he missed two free throws in the closing minutes of the game. Of course, Cole would not even have been in the regional finals if it were not for Shaq, but that didn't make him feel any better. The bottom line to Shaq was that his team lost and he had let them down. Shaq worked hard over the summer, as did his teammates, in an effort to improve and go further in the state tournament the next year. Shaq would often daydream about being an NBA star, giving autographs and having his own named basketball shoe. At the same time he was often frightened of not making it as a basketball star. These doubts made him work hard, and he continued to develop his strength as well as his game.

In the fall of 1988 (Shaq's senior year), the Cole High School team began practice with one goal in mind, winning the 3A basketball championship. Early in the season Shaq was invited to a tournament that showcased the top high school players on a team representing San Antonio. Because of his small school and only recent return to the United States, many basketball "insiders" were unaware of him and his talent. Future NBA players such as Kenny Anderson (who played one year at Georgia Tech before signing with the NBA), Allan Houston (a future star with Tennessee and the New York Knicks), and Jimmy Jackson (later at Ohio State and the Dallas Mavericks) were all at the tournament; but Shaquille, in his words, "tore up the competition." No longer was he unknown and the scholarship offers began to pour in. Shaq visited a number of schools before finally making his choice at the early NCAA signing period in November of his senior year.

At first he had considered 20 schools, then 10, including Louisiana State University (LSU), Louisville, North Carolina, University of Nevada at Las Vegas, Illinois, North Carolina State, and Northwestern. Shaq cancelled his trip to Northwestern after visiting some of the other schools. He really liked Illinois, then coached by Lou Henson, but the cold climate and the distance from his family proved too much for him. Phil's choice was North Carolina (UNC), but he didn't tell his son that because he wanted Shaq to make his own decision. When he met with legendary North Carolina coach, Dean Smith, Smith pulled a list of players out of his pocket. These were former UNC players who had been All-America players and gone on to the NBA. Rather than impress Shaquille, it turned him off. Shaq didn't want to be just another player on a list; he wanted to be judged for his unique abilities.

And then there was Dale Brown, the coach who had first met Shaquille in Germany three years earlier. Brown had lost contact with Shaquille after they moved from Germany, but he contacted one of Shaquille's aunts in Newark and reconnected with him. All of the coaches recruiting him, except for Brown, said that Shaq would start right away. Brown said that Shaquille's own hard work on the court and in the classroom would determine whether he would start. Shaq appreciated the challenge and Brown's honesty, characteristics that he had experienced from their first meeting. He also liked that LSU was only a six-hour automobile drive from San Antonio, so he finally decided on attending LSU in Baton Rouge, Louisiana. One other factor might have been that the girl Shaq was dating in high school had decided to attend Xavier University of Louisiana, located in New Orleans.

There was still a season to be played and a championship to be won, but for Shaq, the dilemma of where to attend college had been solved. Shaq's long summer practice hours and those of his teammates began paying dividends almost immediately, as the team started undefeated and remained that way through 34 games and into the state finals. Shaq was also considerably stronger, having been put on a weight-training regimen by Coach Dave Madura. Shaq was the obvious focus of every squad that the Cole team played and he responded with a dominant season. He had excellent support from his teammates who had to respond with making jump shots when teams collapsed on O'Neal inside with three or even four players. Responding to the challenge, the Cole team led high schools in their district in three-point shooting, making 40 percent of their shots. This made teams unsure of whom to guard and the result was always a Cole victory.

The Cole coaches acknowledged how Shaq had mastered the fundamentals needed by a complete player, but they also told him that they did not want him far from the basket—ever. On offense, his jump shot, although good, was discouraged because it meant that he was not in position for a rebound. So his game emphasized dunking and the coaches encouraged that. He was 6'11", and there were very few other players that tall and none with Shaq's strength. He was, indeed, dominant, dunking with force whenever he got the opportunity in a game. Shaq's mere presence on offense and defense became totally intimidating, and he could recognize the fear in the eyes of his opponents with his first slam dunk in a game. Cole and Shaq were so dominant and his dunks so overwhelming that in one game, where Cole had an enormous lead, the opposing team started throwing the ball in to him just to see him dunk, according to one of the assistant coaches.[3]

As the season unfolded, Cole breezed through game after game with wins, until early in the second half of the season when they played an undefeated team from Karnes City, Texas, and were losing at the half by five points. They tied the score at the end of the third period and went on to win by more than a dozen points. The state tournament found Cole playing Liberty Hill, once again, in the regional finals, and Shaq was determined to erase the memory of the previous year's loss. The victory over Liberty Hill sent Shaq and the Cole High School team into the state semifinals against a team from Hearne, located about 100 miles from San Antonio, in the sparsely populated triangle formed by San Antonio, Dallas, and Houston. Shaq was overwhelming in the game, scoring 38 of his team's 69 points in a 69–56 victory. He also had 20 rebounds, but the game had been close until the end, when O'Neal hit four straight jumpers to allow Cole to pull away to victory.

The State 3A Championship, played at the Erwin Center in Austin on the University of Texas campus, would pit Cole against a team from Clarksville, a community in northeastern Texas, not far from the Oklahoma and Arkansas borders. Clarksville was 29 and 2, while Cole was 35 and 0; and the game was tight the whole way, in part because Shaquille picked up four fouls (five means elimination from the game at all levels, other than professional) with almost seven minutes left in the game and his team leading by eight points. Shaq was forced to sit out for a time and in just two minutes, Clarksville cut the Cole lead to one point, whereupon O'Neal reentered the game, with instructions from Coach Madura not to foul, no matter how tempting it was to try to block a Clarksville shot. Upon his return, Cole scored eight points in a row and finally defeated Clarksville, 68–60, to finish the season undefeated and Class 3A champions. They were the only undefeated high school team in Texas at any level of play.

It was an exciting, emotional time for Shaquille, his teammates, and the entire Cole High School community, but it was not quite over for Shaquille. At the end of the year, various all-state and player-of-the-year honors were awarded, and Shaquille received a number of them. The All–State teams were picked for all five (there are now six) Texas classes, and Shaquille was not only selected for the first team in Class 3A but was also chosen as the 3A player of the year. Shaquille completed his senior high school season averaging 29.9 points, 21.9 rebounds, 9.8 blocked shots, and 2.7 assists per game. He also shot 70 percent from the field, which was being submitted for national recognition, seemingly second only to Bill Walton's shooting percentage when he attended Helix High in California. Shaq also received the ultimate praise from his coach, Dave Madura, who said, "He's the most unselfish kid I've ever seen with that kind of ability. He's a complete team man. He's real popular in school and is easy-going."[4]

Despite coming from a small school and being relatively unknown, Shaquille was selected for the McDonald's High School All-America basketball game, which at the time operated as a showcase for graduating players as they enter college. Until 2005, when the NCAA restricted the entry of players directly out of high school, many players used it as the "jumping off point" to the professional ranks. The game has traditionally emphasized offense, as do most all-star games do, no matter what the level of play.

This is also a venue where many of the shoe companies try to get "chummy" with the future stars in the hopes that they'll sign endorsement contracts with their company as soon as their college eligibility has been completed. Shaq recalls that Nike representatives were there giving out new shoes, sweats, and other paraphernalia to the top players in the country, but Shaq was not really seen as one of them. Most of these players had been tracked since junior high school and played in summer all-star games for a number of years. Because Shaq had been in Europe and then quietly transferred to a small Texas high school, he was largely unknown. Much to his chagrin he was given a pair of what he called "raggedy green Nikes."[5] Then he approached Dick Vitale (a former coach at the University of Detroit, the Detroit Pistons and a well-known basketball commentator) and said, "Mr. Vitale, remember this name: Shaquille O'Neal." Shaq was determined to show what he could do.

The next day (April 23, 1989) at the nationally televised game, Shaquille blocked a shot soon after the opening tip-off, retrieved the ball, and dribbled all the way down court before dunking over three players. This sent Vitale into one of his frenzied exclamations, yelling, "Dale Brown, you've got a diaper dandy in Shaquille O'Neal." The rest of the game was similar and Shaquille scored 18 points, pulling down 16 rebounds and sharing the most valuable player (MVP) award with Bobby Hurley (who went on to lead Duke to three Final Four appearances and set an NCAA record for assists in a career). Shaq's West team defeated Hurley's East team, 112–103. In another high school all-star game, the Dapper Dan Roundball Classic, Shaquille was again the MVP for the West team.

In May Shaquille graduated from Cole and prepared to leave later in the summer for Baton Rouge. His parents were proud of his basketball, but even more of the man that Shaq had become. Both they and he expected him to make them even prouder by becoming the first college graduate in the family. As usual Phil and Lucille set high expectations for their "little warrior" and he intended to respond appropriately.

NOTES

1. Ken Rappoport, *Shaquille O'Neal* (Indianapolis: Walker and Company, 1994), 13–14.

2. Ibid., 17.

3. B. Castello, Matt Marsom, and Nick Rousso, *Shaquille O'Neal* (Lincolnwood, IL: Publications International, Ltd.), 1993.

4. Neal Farmer, "Even Army Can't Stop O'Neal/Named Chronicle Boys' Player of Year;" *Houston Chronicle.com*, April 2, 1989.

5. Shaquille O'Neal, *Shaq Talks Back* (New York: St. Martin's Press, 2001), 31.

Chapter 3

COLLEGE MAN

Baton Rouge is the capital of Louisiana, but it is not a large city, with a population of just over 225,000. That is just a bit more than the 200,000 that it had when Shaq arrived on campus in the fall of 1989. The city is the second largest city in Louisiana, behind New Orleans which is located 90 miles downriver, near the mouth of the Mississippi River. Louisiana is unique in many ways. Although racial segregation was the law of Louisiana from the early part of the twentieth century, there was much more contact between blacks and whites in Louisiana than in any other southern state. Attitudes were a bit different because of Louisiana's different heritage and culture. Settled by the French, Louisiana had a legal system that continued to be more French than British, with Napoleonic law the system in the state, rather than English common law. The Napoleonic Code was instilled when the French Emperor, Napoleon, decreed it for the French possession of Louisiana, which had been ruled for almost 40 years before France gained control. These and other vestiges of French rule made a tradition of racial harmony and acceptance more common in southern Louisiana than in almost every other area of the South.

The closer to New Orleans one was, the less extreme were racial attitudes. In Baton Rouge there was segregation, but attitudes were not as severe as in northern Louisiana and most of the other southern states. Louisiana State University had been integrated as early as 1875 during Reconstruction, but by the end of the nineteenth century, the university had again become totally white. In 1953, LSU accepted its first black undergraduate, but that student left before the end of his freshman year.

In 1964, six African American undergraduates enrolled and the university became more and more integrated.

In 1954, the case of *Brown v. Board of Education of Topeka, Kansas* was decided by the U.S. Supreme Court, and the principle of "separate, but equal" was declared inherently unequal and overturned by that Court. Nevertheless, there was great reluctance on the part of many southern institutions to fully integrate, if at all. Many southern state universities refused to allow African Americans to attend. These included the University of Mississippi, the University of Arkansas, the University of Georgia, and the University of Alabama. Even when a university might have been willing to accept African Americans, some segregationist governors prevented that from happening without the intervention of federal troops.

Although neither Louisiana nor LSU was the site of such actions, acceptance of African Americans was slow to occur in any great numbers at any southern university. Even when this occurred, African Americans did not appear on many southern university athletic teams, because these predominantly white institutions simply would not recruit them. Through most of the 1960s, the largest southern athletic conferences— the Southeastern, Southwest, and Atlantic Coast Conferences—were not only all white, but most of the teams in these conferences would not even schedule games against teams with African Americans on them.

LSU was in the Southeastern Conference where there were no African American basketball players until 1968, when Perry Wallace became a member of the Vanderbilt University basketball team. In 1956, the Louisiana legislature had passed a law "barring interracial sports within the state and by the state's universities when playing outside Louisiana."[1] That law was found unconstitutional in 1958, and the LSU Board of Supervisors abolished the law in 1961. It took until 1969, however, before LSU integrated its sports teams and until 1971 when Collis Temple Jr. became the first African American basketball player at LSU. Thus only 15 years after Temple graduated, Shaquille arrived on campus. By the time of Shaq's arrival, LSU had increased its minority (almost all African American) enrollment to just over 20 percent, and their athletic teams, particularly the high-profile sports of football and men's and women's basketball, were represented by a large percentage of African Americans.

Although Shaq had been heavily recruited by dozens of schools throughout the United States, there were still vestiges of discrimination among people in Baton Rouge and Louisiana. Shaq had been in San Antonio, Texas, one of the most cosmopolitan of American cities, for two years, so he had not experienced much discrimination, although he was aware of it from his short time in Georgia. For most of the Baton Rouge community, Shaq would be an immediate "ray of sunshine" with his gigantic smile and his thunderous dunks. He would be embraced by almost anyone who knew of him. And it would be hard not to recognize him since there were few, if any other, 6'11", 250-pound African Americans in the city. And that made Shaq immediately recognizable throughout the campus and the city. He was often greeted by strangers on campus, as well as in downtown Baton Rouge.

Many underage students try successfully to drink at local establishments, but 17-year-old Shaq would not be one of them. He was simply too prominent. He often accompanied his teammates when they went out to drink, but his role was mostly that of designated driver. He recalled often driving his teammates home in their cars, then having to walk back to the dorm where he lived. Shaq did not drink alcohol and that is still true today. He also didn't smoke or use illegal drugs, reflecting the admonitions of his parents. He enjoyed school and got good grades his freshman year, ending up with a 3.0 grade point average on a 4.0 scale.

Not that Shaq didn't have fun. He had two turntables in his room in the football/basketball athletic dormitory and often played rap music loudly. He liked to dance, although his break dancing days were behind him. For the first time Shaquille began regularly dating various girls. In high school he had been awkward because of his growth spurts, and he didn't spend enough time in any one school to have any long-lasting friendships until the latter part of his senior year. Also, he was a year younger than his classmates. By the time he entered college, he had matured emotionally to "catch up" with his physical maturity and size. One of the reasons that he liked LSU, according to Shaq, was that he noticed all the "beautiful light-skinned Creole girls" on campus. (Creole refers to both a language mix of French and African languages and a person of mixed African and French descent in Louisiana.) He was still dating his girlfriend from high school who was at Xavier, but that relationship ended sometime in his first year at LSU.

Before the basketball season started, Shaq would often drive back to San Antonio on weekends to visit his family. Once the season started, they traveled to almost all of his home games and many away games.

The LSU basketball team was favored to win the rugged Southeastern Conference basketball title in 1989–1990. The previous season the Tigers had won 20 games and lost 12 and almost all of their starters were returning. The star of the team was Chris Jackson, a 6'1" guard from Gulfport, Mississippi. As a freshman Jackson averaged 30.2 points per game, a new NCAA record for freshmen. He also shot more than any other player at a major college in the country. Also returning for the Tigers were Wayne Sims, who had averaged 13 points per game, and Vernel Singleton, a 6'6" center, who averaged 10.8 points per game, but would now return to his natural position of forward. Shaquille, who had now grown to 7'1", would be joined by another big and talented player, Stanley Roberts. Roberts, 7'0", had been academically ineligible his first year, but would be paired with Shaquille in a "twin towers" setting. Also joining the team was Maurice Williamson, another player who had had academic problems the prior year, but who had averaged nearly 40 points per game in high school. The only real loss for LSU was in leadership because of the departure of senior Ricky Blanton, who had averaged 20 points per game. The Tigers appeared loaded and many basketball observers saw them as a potential Final Four team. One magazine even predicted that they would win the national championship. Most basketball magazines picked them to finish in the top 10 in the nation, and Chris Jackson was named by most as a preseason All-America player.

The season opened with relatively easy games. The opening game was against Southern Mississippi, a 91–80 victory for LSU as Jackson had 37 points. Shaquille had 10 points and 5 rebounds in only 16 minutes of play. He was still learning where to play on the court and to keep out of foul trouble. In a one-sided game against Lamar, which LSU won by 40 points, Shaquille got 26 points and 17 rebounds and blocked 6 shots. Still, his play was inconsistent, and he and Roberts did not work well together. Thus Coach Brown would start one or the other and see who would play better. The LSU offense was basically Chris Jackson controlling the ball and often shooting. Shaq's role on offense was to set screens, get rebounds, and put the ball right back up, usually for a dunk. It was frustrating for him and he was benched more than once by Dale Brown, mostly because of his penchant for picking up fouls quickly (Shaq fouled out of nine games that year) or his lack of shooting touch. In addition Brown wanted Shaquille to do more than dunk. For most freshmen, Shaq's play would have been seen as exceptional, but as he was being touted as the best center to come out of high school in many years, the expectations were simply too high to achieve. Shaq began to find a rhythm and became more confident when the Southeastern Conference began play in January. The Tigers had 21 wins in 26 games, and they were 11 and 4 in conference play (tied for the lead) by the end of February.

One highlight in February was a contest in Baton Rouge against Loyola Marymount, a "run-and-gun" team led by All-America players Hank Gathers and Bo Kimble. They scored 48 and 32 points, respectively, and Chris Jackson had 34 points for LSU as they won by a score of 148 to 141.

Shaq had 20 points and 24 rebounds and blocked 12 shots, the most that any Southeastern Conference player had ever had in a game. Still Brown was frustrated with his team's play, which would be dominant, then suddenly "go to sleep." The end of the season resembled the latter mode, rather than the former.

The Tigers lost two of their last three league games to finish tied for second with Alabama at 12 and 6. They lost their first game in the conference tournament, then played in the NCAA Tournament. In their first-round game, the Tigers defeated Villanova, 70 to 63. Shaq had 12 points and 11 rebounds. They then lost their second-round game to Georgia Tech (who went on to the Final Four) and their star freshman guard, Kenny Anderson, 94 to 91. In that game Shaquille scored 19 points, had 14 rebounds, and had four blocked shots.

Despite improving from the previous year, it was a disappointing season for Brown and the Tigers. Nevertheless, Shaquille was named to the first team in the Southeastern Conference and was third on the team in scoring (13.9 points per game) behind Jackson's 27.8 points per game and Roberts' 14.1. Shaquille also led the conference and was ninth in the nation with 12 rebounds per game and he blocked 115 shots (3.6 per game).

Before the next season began, Dale Brown asked both Bill Walton and Kareem Abdul-Jabbar, former UCLA All-America players and NBA All-Pros a number of years, to come to Baton Rouge to work with Shaquille. Brown wanted Shaquille to expand his offense, improve his footwork at center, develop a better hook shot, and improve his jump shot.

During the summer, Shaquille was selected to participate in the U.S. Olympic Festival basketball competition in Minneapolis. Despite scoring only nine points in the championship contest, which his team won, Shaq also had 14 rebounds, 10 blocks, and 6 assists. In four games O'Neal had 98 points and 58 rebounds, both Olympic Festival records, showing why he would be considered for player of the year-honors in the upcoming season. One reporter was almost as impressed with Shaquille's off-court demeanor as he was his on-court performance. William C. Rhoden of the *New York Times* found Shaq thoughtful, almost gentle, but confident, and noted that his conversation frequently revolved around his parents.[2] The rest of the summer Shaq played pick-up games for three hours a day and did calf raises in his room each night to strengthen his legs. The result was an eight-inch improvement in his vertical jump to 36 inches. He also worked construction for a Baton Rouge company to bulk up other areas of his body.

LSU would be seriously considered for top team in the country because all the Tiger starters would be returning; however, by the opening day of practice, the situation had changed dramatically. In the spring, Chris Jackson declared that he would be available for the NBA draft and was the first draft pick of the Denver Nuggets in the June draft. Stanley Roberts continued to have academic difficulties and flunked out of school. He ended up playing the next season in a professional league in Spain and eventually returned to the United States to play for a number of NBA teams. He never became a star and was eventually out of the league for the same behavior that he had exhibited at LSU. Roberts was not very motivated and it showed on the floor in his lackadaisical play. When, for some reason, he *was* motivated, his play was often spectacular, but those times were too rare for a professional team to have enough patience to tolerate. In addition, Stanley Roberts liked to eat and his increased weight negatively affected his mobility and endurance.

SHAQ'S SOPHOMORE YEAR AT LSU

After a summer of playing basketball and working construction, Shaquille returned to fall practice at LSU in great shape. He had gained muscle mass, increased his vertical jump, and was eager to improve his and the team's play. According to his own assessment of his freshman year: "I made a lot of mistakes and fouled too much. I think I'll be better with a year behind me."[3] Almost every basketball poll placed LSU in the top 20 in the nation, and they also had Shaquille tabbed as an All-America player. He was selected by the Southeastern Conference Media corps as the preseason player of the year in the Southeastern Conference. Shaquille was on the cover of at least eight preseason magazines, but he maintained his humility. His teammates noted that he was shy off the court and he took all the attention in stride. LSU was picked to either win or be second to Alabama in the conference. The Tigers had lost Jackson and Roberts, but they had gained Mike Hansen, a point guard who transferred from the University of Tennessee-Martin and had scored 40 points against LSU two seasons before.

With the departure of both Chris Jackson and Stanley Roberts, there was no question that Shaquille was "the man" for LSU basketball, and his new status brought him new-found popularity and more dates with more girls. He was having so much fun dating that he felt he was "paying back every girl who shot me down earlier in life." Then he fell hard for a girl who was dating lots of other guys, mostly football players, behind his back. When Shaq found out how he'd been taken advantage of and was being made the butt of so many jokes, he was crushed. His mother told him to stop playing around with girls and he changed his behavior. No longer would he hurt girls' feeling because he could. Instead he just played it straight and honest with them and he was much happier.

The Tiger basketball team opened the 1990–1991 season at the Tip-Off Classic in Springfield, Massachusetts, site of the Naismith Memorial Basketball Hall of Fame, as well as the invention of the game in 1891. LSU met Villanova University, located in suburban Philadelphia and part of the Big East Conference, an average team that was 18 and 15 the previous year and would end up 17 and 15 in 1990–1991. This was the kind of team that LSU should have brushed aside on its way to the NCAA Tournament, but that did not happen, as Villanova upset the Tigers 93–91. Shaq had 24 points and 11 rebounds, but it was not enough, as the Tigers resorted to the unfocused play that had characterized their prior season. Then, they seemed to awaken from the lethargy and won six straight games, including a 92–82 win in Baton Rouge against the University of Arizona, the Number 2 ranked team in the country, which would finish the year as Number 7 and were 7 and 0. Shaquille had 29 points and 14 rebounds, as well as six blocked shots. In the six-game winning streak, Shaquille averaged 30 points and 16 rebounds per game to show that he was, indeed, the best big man in college. In fact, Lute Olsen, the Arizona head coach, said as much after his team was defeated by LSU.

A big problem for LSU was outside shooting. Unless the Tigers could make opposing teams regret double teaming Shaquille inside by shooting accurate three-point shots outside, he would continue to be guarded by two or three men. This strategy would wear him down and adversely affect LSU's chances of winning. Most of the season, unfortunately, would find Shaquille guarded heavily by multiple players and his teammates unable to hit long shots consistently. Still, he was able to score consistently and led the Tigers in scoring and rebounding in almost every game. In late December LSU lost to the University of Illinois by a 102–96 score, with Shaquille getting 28 points, 12 rebounds, and 7 blocked shots before fouling out. He was double-, triple-, and even quadruple-teamed and this tired him greatly. Being tired and having "heavy legs" often lead to fouling as a player may reach with his arms rather than move his feet on defense.

This method of defending LSU and Shaq was becoming more "popular." To beat LSU, went the theory, a team only had to contain Shaq. That, of course, was easier said than done. In December 1991, Shaquille was the subject of a short piece in *People Weekly*, an unusual honor for a college basketball player. Besides the usual biographical commentary and nice photographs of Shaq, Coach Dale Brown was quoted a saying that Shaq was "close to making the dean's list" this year as a business administration major.[4] Coach Brown was exaggerating a bit, as he often did, but the point was that Shaq was a good student and not at risk of losing his eligibility and leaving school for the pros early, as some top stars frequently did. What was making his remaining in school problematic was the rough play. Shaq's father Phil Harrison was vocal in the media and in complaints to officials regarding the hammering that Shaquille was taking. Phil noted that if Shaquille wasn't having any fun and if his risk of injury became higher, then Shaquille might, indeed, forgo his remaining college eligibility and jump to the NBA the next year. In February Phil Harrison complained directly to the Southeastern Conference Supervisor of Officials, John Guthrie, after a loss at Mississippi State. Phil said that Guthrie agreed that Shaquille's safety had to be protected and that the beatings he was taking would be cleaned up.

By the time the conference season began in January, LSU had won 8 of 10 games, losing only to Villanova and the University of Illinois, and topping Arizona and Loyola Marymount of Los Angeles, as well as a number of overmatched opponents. The Tigers began by winning only five of their eight games in January. In one victory over Vanderbilt, a respected university in Nashville, Tennessee, Shaq scored 34 points and got 11 rebounds, and he was consistently scoring 25 to 30 points in every game while grabbing 12 to 20 rebounds per game and blocking about 5 shots per game.

In February the Tigers played the Duke Blue Devils, the preseason pick as Number 1 in the country. The Blue Devils, located in Durham, North Carolina, are members of the Atlantic Coast Conference and were led by All-America players Bobby Hurley and Christian Laettner, the latter one of the other players (besides Shaq) who was mentioned as a possible player of the year. The game was played in Cameron Indoor Stadium, a cozy gym that held less than 10,000 people and where the Blue Devils had won 63 games in a row against non-Atlantic Coast Conference (ACC) teams. The Duke fans were, and still are, known for being clever with their very pointed and well-orchestrated insults and this game was no exception.

In the first half, Shaquille got into foul trouble guarding Laettner, and he was forced to sit on the bench with two fouls. Shaquille had only four points at the half, his worst showing of the season, as Duke led 48 to 39. The second half did not get much better, as the Duke defenders kept the guards from getting the ball in to Shaquille, who took only nine shots in the entire game, of which he played just 28 minutes because of foul trouble. The LSU team, aside from Shaquille, shot just 35 percent from the field. By contrast, Duke shot 57 percent from the field in Duke's 88 to 70 victory. Laettner had 24 points to lead the Blue Devils, and he also had 11 rebounds to Shaquille's 10. The 9,314 fans in Durham, North Carolina serenaded Shaq with chants of "Overrated." It was a low point of the season for Shaquille.

Shaq continued to play well in the rugged Southeastern Conference, scoring 34 against Georgia (along with 16 rebounds), 28 and 33 points in two games against Kentucky (to go with 17 and 16 rebounds), but LSU finished the league season with a win-loss record of 13 and 5, after losing their last game to Mississippi State. Part of the reason for that loss was that Shaquille sustained a hairline fracture of his left leg in the LSU victory over Florida in late February and missed the regular season finale. The exact cause was unclear, but it was likely that it occurred when he caught a rebound and landed while pivoting on his leg. The torque (twisting power) may have been too much for the leg to sustain. He was then forced to miss the Southeastern Conference tournament as the Tigers lost in the second round.

One pleasant development in early March was that Shaquille was named the Southeastern Conference Player of the Year for 1990–1991, but that was offset somewhat by a new round of rumors that he would leave school at the end of the year and join the NBA the next season. The main reason, once again, was the beating that he was taking on the court. In addition, there was a marked increase in "phantom fouls" being called on Shaquille. Shaq assessed it in this way:

> The refs always assume I did something but there are a lot of ac-
> tors in the Southeastern Conference. I get fouled all the time.
> That's the only way that they can get the ball from me.[5]

Both Coach Brown and Phil Harrison reiterated Shaq's laments, and Phil said that "if Shaq was going to be subjected to such hooliganism from opponents, he wouldn't stand in O'Neal's way if he chose to leave (school) early." (Cotton) Billy Cunningham, the Miami Heat vice-president said, "If he were to come out, he could sign a 10-year contract worth between $40 and $50 million."[6]

Shaq was getting pummeled, but he also was still having fun, especially being a college student. He enjoyed his classes and his friends, and he had a girlfriend. Always intrigued with rap music, he rather fancied himself a disc jockey, spinning records on two turntables in his apartment. His room had NBA posters on the wall and the music and basketball "themes" indicated Shaquille's greatest passions. He had a Ford Bronco that had the license plate, "The Shack Attack." And he loved the attention of being recognized all over campus. A local family even named their child Shaquille Rashaun, after him. Shaq was so honored that when he heard this, he jumped in his car and drove to the home of the new baby with a baby gift. The parents were ecstatic, but not totally surprised; the father said that he knew Shaq would come. He was becoming almost legendary in the region.

After its loss in the SEC Tournament on March 9 to Georgia Tech, LSU was invited to the NCAA tournament, but, with a 20 and 9 record, was seeded only sixth in the Midwest regional. They met the 11th seed, University of Connecticut (U Conn) Huskies in Minneapolis. The higher the seed, the greater likelihood of winning, so LSU was considered the favorite in the contest. The winner would likely play the third seed, but LSU was unable to perform as expected and suffered their worst loss in the NCAA tournament in six years, by a score of 79 to 62. U Conn played a variety of zone defenses against LSU, with a 6'9" player playing in front of Shaq to make passing in to him difficult and another tall player behind him to make lobbing the ball in also a problem.

The solution to this double teaming zone was, again, for the Tigers to hit outside shots, but they shot as poorly as they had all year. Shaquille was 11 of 22 from the field, which is 50 percent, but the rest of the team shot 13 of 53, a woeful 24.5 percent. As Coach Brown noted, "We've been a horrendous shooting team all year long" and this game proved it. In the second half, Connecticut's lead stretched to 61–37 with 11 minutes to go. This loss may have been one reason Shaq considered returning the next year, despite all the rumors that he would not. After the game Shaq said "The end of the season was pretty disappointing, but the good thing about America is that there's always next year."[7] There is no question that Shaquille had to be frustrated by the losses and the inability of his teammates to score from the outside. After all, this collapsing defense had been happening since he was in high school, and his Cole High School team had shooters who hit 40 percent from three point range, so it didn't seem too much to expect something similar from highly recruited college teammates. Because the year had ended so badly and Shaquille was being told that he would be the first player drafted out of college, it still remained to be seen whether he would actually return to LSU to play in the 1991–1992 season.

Two weeks after the loss to U Conn, Shaq told a reporter from the *San Antonio Express-News* that he was likely to remain in school another year. He said, "It's pretty tempting [to go pro], but I don't think that I'm ready yet." He also noted that he was aware that he could lose millions of dollars if he were to suffer a career-ending injury, "but, if I get hurt and can't play basketball anymore, it wasn't meant to be."[8] Shaquille ended the season averaging 27.6 points per game, which was seventh in the nation; 14.7 rebounds per game, first in the nation; and 5.0 blocks per game, third in the nation. He had also improved his always erratic free-throw shooting to just under 64 percent after making only 56 percent of his charity tosses the prior year. *Sports Illustrated,* the Associated Press (AP), and United Press International (UPI) all named him player of the year.

Despite his awards, Shaquille knew that his game was not complete. During his first year in college he had been asked primarily to rebound and play defense. The next year Coach Brown made him a team captain and told Shaq that he had to be a bigger scorer, which was just fine with Shaq. Now he needed to improve his ball handling, defensive movement, shooting range, and his ability to run the floor more consistently. Over the summer he worked on all of those things, as well as trying to improve his strength even more. Shaq wanted to be better and he wanted his Tiger teammates to be better, too. Their goal was to win the Southeastern Conference and to advance in the NCAA tournament. After two years of high goals and great disappointments, their sights would be set a bit more modestly for 1991–1992.

NOTES

1. Russell J. Henderson, "The Mississippi State University Basketball Controversy and the Repeal of the Unwritten Law: Something More Than the Game Will Be Lost," *Journal of Southern History* 68 (1977): 829.

2. William C. Rhoden, "LSU Center Is Making an Impact on the Court," *New York Times,* July 11, 1990, A16.

3. Bill Sullivan, , "O'Neal Is LSU's Only Big Man on Campus Now," *Houston Chronicle,* Nov. 24, 1990, 24.

4. Wm Plummer and Ron Ridenour, "Shaqville," *People Weekly,* December 16, 1991, 142.

5. Anthony Cotton, "The Shaqnificent Mr. O'Neal; LSU Sophomore Beginning to Play, Feel Like 7-foot Jordan. *Washington Post,* Feb. 27, 1991, C1.

6. Dick Weiss, "'Shack' Attacks Life with Zeal, O'Neal Having Fun at LSU," *Chicago Tribune,* Feb. 17, 1991, 9.

7. O'Neal, *Shaq Talks Back,* 152.

8. "O'Neal Likely to Stay at LSU," *Washington Post,* March 28, 1991, B3.

Chapter 4

THE PLAYER
OF THE YEAR RETURNS

Shaquille returned to campus in the fall in great shape, and, at the beginning of preseason practice, Coach Brown noted how he had continued to mature in his approach to the game. In addition Shaquille continued to grow. It is not uncommon for males to have a late growth spurt in their late teens, and he was just 20 when he grew once again, gaining a half inch to an inch in height to about 7'2". Brown noted that team doctors had checked his knees and there were indications from bone scans that Shaquille would grow even more.

No matter what height Shaquille was by this time, the media writers agreed that he was a first team All-America pick, and most selected him as the player of the year for the upcoming season. Other prominent players mentioned on the All-America teams were Christian Laettner of Duke, the team picked to finish Number 1 in the country, Alonzo Mourning of Georgetown, Calbert Cheaney of Indiana, and Jimmy Jackson of Ohio State. In addition LSU was picked to finish in the top 10 in the country by most basketball observers and at least one, the respected *Street & Smith's College/Prep Basketball* magazine, picked them to finish Number 2. Many writers also picked LSU to win the Southeastern Conference title, even though both Kentucky and Arkansas were seen as also being two of the best teams in the country. The league would operate with an Eastern and Western Division because of the addition of two new teams (Arkansas and South Carolina), but many saw the SEC as one of the two strongest conferences (along with the Atlantic Coast Conference) in the country.

Besides Shaquille, who was obviously the key to success for the Tigers, three starters, T. J. Pugh, Vernell Singleton, and Mike Hansen, would be back. The last two had averaged in double figures, but it would be Hansen's outside shooting as well as that of incoming freshmen Paul Marshall and David Mascia, that would lead to a possible conference title for the team. Dale Brown noted, "Our biggest Achilles heel was we couldn't hit from the outside. We think we've corrected that."

Early in the season, Shaq overheard some of the LSU football players say that they were going to beat up one of the LSU basketball players, Clarence Ceasar, a freshman guard, for fooling around with a football player's girlfriend. Trying to be what he called a responsible teammate (and naïve dummy), Shaq said to the football players that he would beat them up also, which was a big mistake. Reconsidering what he said he went to the football captains in the athletic dormitory to try to work out this issue, but a big linebacker on the team was not about to accept diplomacy and challenged Shaquille, asking if he was ready to fight. With that, Shaq punched him in the face and ran out of there as fast as he could. Within five minutes most of the football team was after Shaq, chanting their desire to beat him up. They broke down the door where some of the basketball players lived, and Shaq and the same linebacker were fighting almost immediately. The police were called and when they arrived the football players started beating on them as Shaq, according to him, sneaked out the back. Then the football coach and Dale Brown showed up and they were also ready to fight. All of the football players were arrested, but not any basketball players, and this caused a lot of hard feelings, as some people said that Shaq and the basketball players got special treatment. The result was that the players were kicked out of the dorm and had to find off-campus housing. Shaquille later found this to be useful because he had to learn to budget to pay his bills. But this incident was not an auspicious start to Shaquille's junior season.

Brown had scheduled some very tough nonconference opponents for LSU for 1991–1992. These included the University of Nevada-Las Vegas, the NCAA runners-up the previous year; the University of Arizona; the University of Louisville; the University of Texas; and, once again, Duke, the national champions in 1990–1991. There was no question that Shaq and his teammates would be battle-hardened and weary by the time the season ended and the NCAA Tournament began.

The Tigers did not come out winning as they had the previous year. Of course, there were easy victories over a number of overmatched teams. In November 1991, Shaq's influence on college basketball was so enormous that at the beginning of the season *Sports Illustrated* ran an unusual article called "Shaq Snacks" by Franz Lidz. It was unusual because Shaq was not pictured or really discussed much in the article. Instead it had pictures of seven centers on teams that LSU was due to meet later in the season and was likely to defeat handily. The seven players would have not ever appeared in the national magazine except for their being shown as future "victims" of Shaquille. This was likely the first time any article like this ever appeared in a basketball magazine and, although a gimmick, it did illustrate how far-reaching Shaquille's impact really was. Victories over Northeast Louisiana and Middle Tennessee State came easily. Then LSU traveled to Las Vegas to play UNLV, who was supposed to be having a rebuilding year after losing all five starters from the previous season. Instead, UNLV stunned the Tigers with a convincing 76–55 victory. Shaquille had 26 points but had only 7 rebounds and sat for short stretches in foul trouble. Even when he was playing he was not the aggressive Shaq of the previous year. Shaq was outplayed by Elmore Spencer, who had 20 points and 12 rebounds for UNLV (both career highs). The Tigers did not help themselves by shooting just 31 percent from the field, including only 2 of 16 three-point attempts. They were also outrebounded 55 to 41. Dale Brown summed it up, "They out-hustled us, they outrebounded us. They beat us totally."

The next game, against Arizona, was even worse for LSU and Shaq. The previous year the Tigers had surprised the Wildcats in a surprisingly easy LSU victory in Baton Rouge, but the result in Tucson was much different. Shaq was held to just 10 points and 4 rebounds, and Arizona romped the Tigers by a score of 87 to 67. The game was nationally televised and Shaquille's grandmother, Odessa, called him on the phone to reprimand him for his less than outstanding play. She chided him for showing a decided lack of aggressiveness compared to previous years, and Shaq took her admonitions to heart, at least against some weaker teams. He had 23 points in 24 minutes in a 62-point triumph over Nichols State and 43 points, 19 rebounds, and 8 blocks against Northern Arizona in a 159-86 victory. These were followed, however, by another loss, this time to Louisville by one point, leaving the Tigers at five wins and three losses, and dropping them from the top 10 as they met the University of Texas. Playing in the New Orleans Superdome before 42,000 fans, LSU edged the Longhorns, 84–83, sending Coach Dale Brown into an angry tirade after the game. He blasted his team for another lackluster performance against a team that they should have destroyed easily. Shaq blocked a lay-up attempt with less than 10 seconds left, then recovered the ball to preserve the victory, but Brown was angry at the lack of leadership on his team. The guards had committed a number of turnovers in the second half to help Texas get back in the game, but Brown wanted all of his upperclassmen to share in the blame, including Shaquille, who had scored

19 points and retrieved 19 rebounds. Brown said it was a game that his team did not deserve to win, and he was as mad as he'd ever been about one of his teams.

The Tigers headed into conference play with a record of 6 and 3. After three games in the league, the Tigers were 2 and 1, following a victory over Number 9-ranked Alabama, but LSU, at 8 and 4, was no longer ranked in the top 25 teams in the country. Shaquille's numbers were not much different from the previous year. He was averaging 24 points, nearly 14 rebounds, and 5 blocks per game; but something was missing, and even Shaq acknowledged that. He was taking fewer shots and seemed to be playing "softer," possibly to avoid getting hurt. This renewed the stories that he would leave school at the end of the season, forgoing his senior year, to declare himself eligible for the NBA draft.

LSU ran up four more victories after the Alabama game and then faced Number 14 Kentucky in Baton Rouge on February 2. The Wildcats were sent packing 74 to 53, making LSU 13 and 4 and renewing talk of how good they could be. Others also noted that Kentucky was probably not strong enough to be rated so highly, but, whatever the view, everyone conceded that Shaquille played a great game. In 37 minutes he had 20 points, 20 rebounds, and 6 blocks; but after the game he said, "We're not that good. I think we're mediocre now."[1] For once LSU shot three-point shots well, making 7 of 12 in the first half, and if they could continue like that, the rest of the season looked very bright, indeed.

Six nights later, the Duke Blue Devils, ranked Number 1 in the country came to Baton Rouge to meet the Tigers, who were now 14 and 4 and winners of 11 of their past 12 games. An LSU victory would be enough to get them back into the national title picture, but Duke was able to keep its top ranking by winning 77 to 67. Shaq had better numbers (25 points and 12 rebounds) than Christian Laettner (22 points, 10 rebounds), but Laettner's teammates had more support for him. Duke shot 51 percent from the field, but LSU shot just 41 percent. The percentage without Shaq, however, was only 35 percent and three-point shooting was 33 percent. In addition, Shaq was only three of nine from the free-throw line and just one of six in the last three minutes. He lamented his poor shooting from the line but had no excuses for it. It was a very disappointing loss.

The Tigers played adequately the rest of the season, but not well enough to win the Western Division of the Southeastern Conference, finishing second to Arkansas. LSU was 12 and 4 in the league to the Razorbacks' 13 and 3. Kentucky won the Eastern Division with a 12 and 4 record.

In the Southeastern Conference tournament, LSU was leading Tennessee by a score of 73 to 51 with just over 10 minutes left. At that point

Carlus Groves of Tennessee grabbed Shaquille around the waist and pulled backward as he was heading to dunk the ball. Once a player is in the air, it is difficult to maintain equilibrium if he is pulled in this manner and severe injury could result. Shaquille was angry, both about the incident and the continual beating that he was getting each game. This time, rather than just taking it, he snapped. Shaquille swung at Groves and challenged him. Groves swung at Shaq. Both were restrained, but the fight escalated as players from both teams rushed the floor in defense of their teammates. Dale Brown was also on the floor trying to punch Groves who also tried to do the same to Brown. Fights broke out all over the court, and it took nearly a half-hour to restore order. Five players from each team were ejected and Shaquille was suspended for the next game, which was the semifinal contest of the SEC tournament. Groves received a similar suspension, but it was only enforceable if Tennessee got a post-season tournament bid. Coach Brown received only a reprimand, which some people thought was too lenient for an action by a role model, which a coach is to his players. LSU won the game 99–89, and Shaq finished with 16 points and 16 rebounds, despite missing the last 10 minutes of the contest.

Without Shaquille, the Tigers lost to Kentucky, 80–74, in the next game. Kentucky went on to the NCAA East Region finals where they lost to Duke on a miracle shot by Christian Laettner with one second left in the game. Duke went on to win the NCAA tournament.

Shaquille and LSU were invited to the NCAA tournament, specifically the Western regional in Boise, Idaho. They were seeded seventh and faced 12th seeded Brigham Young University in the first round. Sensing that he might be ending his college career soon, Shaquille literally rose to the occasion and set an NCAA tournament record with 11 blocks to lead the Tigers to a 94 to 83 victory. Shaq also scored 26 points and took down 13 rebounds. His teammates helped greatly, as the Tigers shot 51 percent from the field, including 63 percent in the second half.

By winning, the Tigers won the right to face the Number 2 seed Indiana Hoosiers, coached by Bobby Knight. Indiana was 24 and 6 and had finished second to Jimmy Jackson's Ohio State team in the rugged Big Ten conference. Knight and Dale Brown had a long history of animosity toward each other. Knight had often disparaged Brown's coaching ability, and Brown thought Knight was just a bully with fans, players and referees alike. So the game meant a lot to both coaches besides the obvious, which meant that one team moved on and the other was eliminated from the NCAA tournament. With Shaquille strongly rumored to be leaving school and playing in the NBA the next year, this game may have been his last opportunity to get to an NCAA Final Four. Shaq had been seen as "going through the motions" early in the season, but now he had shown how determined he was to win and overcome all the physical and verbal abuse that he had been taking throughout his career.

The Tigers came out hot and burst into a 27 to 14 lead 10 minutes into the game behind the hot shooting of Maurice Williamson and Clarence Ceasar, but Indiana, led by Alan Henderson and Calbert Cheaney, came back to catch the Tigers and led 45 to 38 at the half. Shaquille had only nine points at halftime, but he started getting the ball down low in the second half and his shots were falling. He scored nine points in the first two minutes of the second half and the game was tied at 47. Four times, Shaq had three-point plays where he made the basket, was fouled while shooting, and converted the free throw. In fact, free throws, his usual weak spot, were, instead, his strong point as he made 12 of 12 from the free-throw line.

The Hoosiers pulled away again and led 69–59 with eight minutes to play before LSU rallied to close the lead to three points with four minutes remaining. That was as close as the Tigers would come. When Dale Brown pulled him from the game with a minute left and LSU down by 10, Shaquille got a standing ovation from the Boise, Idaho fans. He had scored 36 points, grabbed 12 rebounds, and blocked 5 shots, but it was not enough as Indiana won 89 to 79. He also had been grabbed, held, and hacked throughout the game.

Dale Brown said after the game that he had noted when he left his hotel that morning that the winner of this game would win the national championship. When Bobby Knight was told of this comment, he responded with his usual lack of grace, extending the ill feelings between him and Brown. Knight said, "Had he been drinking? Were his eyes glazed over?"[2] It turned out that Brown was only a bit off as Indiana went to the Final Four before losing to eventual champion, Duke, 81 to 78, in the national semifinals.

As for Shaquille, he put a towel over his head and hung it down, probably shedding a few tears for what might have been. After the game Brown said that he would recommend that O'Neal leave school if the NCAA did not adopt a more severe penalty for intentional fouls. That penalty was two shots and retention of the ball, but, even that was hardly called. When asked about Brown's comment, Shaquille said that he would make a decision sometime before May regarding whether to turn pro for the next year.

Shaquille's final totals for his junior year were similar to the previous season. He scored 24.1 points, took down 14.0 rebounds, and blocked 5.2

shots per game and was a unanimous All-America player. He was player of the year, once again, in the Southeastern Conference. In three years and five NCAA tournament games against the toughest competition, he averaged 24.0 points, 13.2 rebounds, and 6.0 blocks per game. He also averaged 77.3 percent on his free-throw shooting. Shaquille set the Southeastern Conference record for blocks in a season three straight years from 115 in 1990 to 140 in 1991 to 157 in 1992. He led the league in rebounding three straight years and was the first player since Charles Barkley (of Auburn) to do this. He had 73 double-doubles at LSU (games in which he had double figures in both scoring and rebounding).

SHAQ GRADUATES TO THE NBA

Two weeks later, on April 3, the question about Shaquille's status for the next season was answered at a press conference held at Ft. Sam Houston in San Antonio, where Phil Harrison was still based. Shaq had gone home to talk the decision over with his mother and father, and both they and his siblings were by his side when he announced that he would not return to LSU, but would make himself available for the NBA draft in June. Shaq said that he felt it was time for a change and time for him to move on. He also said that he would withdraw from LSU the next week, but that he would return at some point to complete his degree. He carried a 2.9 grade point average as a business administration major, and he was planning to capitalize on his expertise in his major as he became a professional. Nevertheless both of his parents had been adamant in their wanting him to be the first in the family to earn a college degree, and he had promised his parents that he would do so. (He did complete his degree in 2000).

Shaquille noted that he was not making his decision out of anger or frustration, although he conceded that having three or four men surrounding him often limited his ability to show all of his basketball talents. He said that he hadn't had much fun playing at LSU in 1991–1992, and his father had said that if he wasn't having fun at what he was doing, it was time to do something else. Playing in the NBA would be "something else," something at which he was determined to succeed, and nearly every observer agreed he would. Despite his disappointment at Shaquille's decision, Phil agreed with him. He said that he "saw guys knee him in the crotch, elbow him, shove him and then heard the refs say that he was big and strong and could take it. Well, he doesn't have to take it."[3]

Shortly thereafter Shaquille moved to Los Angeles where he lived in a rented apartment and worked out with professionals in the area on a daily basis, including Magic Johnson. Shaq liked L.A. a lot and hoped, initially, that some sort of deal might be worked out so that he would end up playing for the Lakers.

Speculation began immediately regarding who would draft him and how much it would cost to sign him to a contract. It was predicted that he would be the highest paid rookie in NBA history, with a likely $5 million per year salary. Amid that speculation, Shaquille received more honors for his basketball play. In late April, three weeks after his announcement that he was turning pro, he received the James J. Corbett Award given annually to Louisiana's outstanding amateur athlete. During this same time, Shaquille had signed a contract with a Los Angeles-based agent named Leonard Amato.

LEONARD AMATO

The choice of Leonard Amato was a shrewd one by Shaquille. He heard the pitches of a number of agents, but he felt very comfortable with Armato, who coach Dale Brown had introduced him to, and with what Armato seemed to be able to do for Shaquille. Together they devised a plan that would market Shaquille as a commodity, and they formed a corporation almost immediately to identify Shaquille as a "product." The June draft was likely to find Shaquille as either the first or second draft pick, and the pair began preparing for that by seeking contracts with various product lines for Shaquille to represent.

Armato, himself, was a former outstanding basketball player at the University of the Pacific in Stockton, California in the 1970s and, at one time, represented Michael Jackson as well as Kareem Abdul-Jabbar, the NBA's all time leading scorer; Ronnie Lott of the San Francisco 49ers; and Hakeem Olajuwon. In college Armato was the top free-throw shooter in the Pacific Coast Athletic Association, the league in which Pacific competed and he was coached by Stan Morrison, who later coached at the University of Southern California from 1979 to 1986. Shaquille liked Leonard because he didn't make any wild promises like many prospective agents did. He said that he came from a good family and wanted to do things "the right way".

So Shaquille decided that he would let Leonard Armato represent him. When he was about to sign a contract with Shaq, Phil Harrison told Leonard that if he messed with Shaq, he (Phil) would kill him. Leonard laughed a little nervously, but Lucille said, "he's serious," and he was. Not that Leonard had any intention of "stiffing" his client. Instead he had plans for Shaq to be marketed as Shaq, his own corporation, and Shaq and

Leonard worked out plans for Shaquille to be prominent in commercial enterprises of various types. The first two contracts were with Reebok for more than $2 million and one with the team that would draft Shaquille— and that remained to be seen.

NOTES

1. William Reed, "Beware! Shaq Is Back," *Sports Illustrated* 76 (5): 1992, 28–29.

2. "Indiana Turns Back LSU's Shaq Attack," *St. Louis Post Dispatch*, March 22, 1992, 3F.

3. Phil Taylor, "The Grand Prize," *Sports Illustrated*, 76 (May 18, 1992): 42.

Chapter 5

THE PROFESSIONAL: SHAQ IS MAGIC

To try to keep the league competitive, the NBA conducts an annual draft of players who are eligible for the league the next year. At one time those eligible were college players whose class had graduated, but, over time, eligibility extended to anyone who declared himself wishing to play in the NBA or whose college eligibility had ended or who were playing internationally. Players then were limited to negotiating with only one team. The order of the draft initially had been in reverse order from the way the teams had finished, but, in 1985, the NBA decided to add another element to the draft. A lottery would be held about a month before the actual draft among the teams that did not make the playoffs.

Initially the lottery was set up so that all nonplayoff teams had an equal chance at the top pick, but in 1990, the lottery was altered to favor the teams with the worst records the previous year, but it still would be possible for a team with the best record who did not make the playoffs to earn the right to draft first. Thus in 1992, the team with the greatest likelihood of getting the Number 1 pick was the Minnesota Timberwolves, a team that had won only 15 games the year before. The next most likely was the Orlando Magic, which had won 21 games. These two expansion teams had begun play just three years before, and neither had ever made the playoffs nor had they ever won more than 31 games in a season.

The NBA lottery was held on May 17, 1992, and 11 teams were involved. Almost everyone agreed that Shaquille was the top player in the draft if a team could adjust its payroll to sign him. This was necessary because of the NBA agreement with the players that capped the total team salary, thereby preventing the richest (and often the teams with the best records) teams from outspending the other teams to maintain their dominance. By the time the representatives of the 11 teams got together with NBA Commissioner David Stern, the lottery itself had already been held under the supervision of a major accounting firm, and the results were top secret. Stern held 11 large envelopes with numbers on them from 1 to 11, each with the logo of the team that would get that number pick in the draft.

The first envelope opened, which meant that the team that got the 11th pick in the draft was Houston. Following that in order were Atlanta, Philadelphia, Milwaukee, Sacramento, and Washington. The number five pick went to Denver, leaving Dallas and Charlotte as well as Minnesota and Orlando. The next envelope had the logo of the Mavericks, leaving just three teams in the "Shaquille sweepstakes." To the great disappointment of the Timberwolves, they were selected next. After a pause of a few minutes, Commissioner Stern tore open another envelope and revealed the logo of the Charlotte Hornets. The Number one pick belonged to the Orlando Magic and their General Manager Pat Williams.

Pat Williams had been an NBA executive for more than 20 years, starting with the Philadelphia 76ers, and had already experienced trying to build a team as the first general manager of the Chicago Bulls, beginning in the 1970s. He had also been the general manager of the Atlanta Hawks before becoming president and general manager of the Magic. In three seasons the Magic had not developed any winning tradition and had no real "franchise" player around which a team could be built. That would all change if the Magic and Williams could succeed in signing Shaquille.

There was a huge incentive for the Magic to sign O'Neal swiftly. In anticipation of Shaquille's presence on the team, fans in the Orlando region had already begun calling to purchase season tickets, and within a week more than 500 were sold. Williams said, "We'll get him signed. Everyone wants to come to Orlando."[1] Shaquille's initial comments seemed to indicate that Williams was right. In a statement issued by Leonard Armato, Shaq said:

> I am thrilled that Orlando Magic's General Manager, Pat Williams, was so excited and sincere about the possibility of having me on the team. I was particularly happy to see the people of Orlando so complimentary towards me. I am excited about my upcoming career in the NBA. Soon I will sit down with my family and my attorney to formulate a game plan.[2]

Of course, Shaquille hadn't even officially been drafted yet, but Pat Williams left no doubt that he would be their pick:

Ultimately in this league, you win with special players like Dr. J (Julius Erving), Kareem (Abdul-Jabbar), Larry Bird or Magic Johnson. I get the sense that O'Neal is a special player. He's only 20-years-old and not finished offensively, but on ability, potential, size and power, he's the class of the draft.[3]

SIGNING SHAQ

The draft was held on June 24 and, to no one's surprise, Orlando drafted Shaquille as the Number one pick. That choice was followed by Charlotte selecting Alonzo Mourning from Georgetown; Minnesota taking Christian Laettner of Duke, and Dallas opting for Jimmy Jackson of Ohio State. As promised, Pat Williams set out to sign Shaquille as quickly as possible. To achieve that goal, he had to restructure his payroll to fit under the cap. The Magic had $1.2 million that they could work with, but to sign Shaq to a $3 million contract for the first year (and a $39.9 million contract for seven years), they would have to find a way to shed $1.8 million in contracts that were with their current players. In late July a new element, time, entered into the picture when Stanley Roberts, Shaq's old LSU teammate, who had just completed his rookie year with Orlando, signed an offer sheet with Dallas for $14.7 million for five years. This meant that Roberts would go to Dallas unless the Magic matched the offer within 15 days.

The 15 days were also important to Shaquille's contract. If the Magic didn't sign Shaquille first, then Roberts's new contract would count against the salary cap, and it would be impossible to sign Shaq without cutting essential players from the team. So Pat Williams had two weeks to get changes in current contracts and sign Shaquille, or they would lose Roberts, who had averaged just over 10 points and 6 rebounds a game his first year in the league. Williams got Keith Glass, the agent for three players—Greg Kite, Scott Skiles, and Jerry Reynolds—to agree to cuts in all their contracts that totaled $630,000. Glass explained that he wasn't doing this because he was a nice guy, but noted that signing Shaq meant that the team would be more successful and that would mean that his clients would ultimately stand the chance to get more money by making the playoffs and because the club would probably pay them more in the future. Another player, Terry Catledge, also agreed to a cut of $330,000 in his salary, but those changes got only the Magic halfway to its goal. These arrangements took almost the entire two weeks. Then Williams was able to trade another player, Sam Vincent, which cleared another $600,000 from the cap. Finally, just two days before the deadline, the Magic gave up their rights to Sean Higgins and saved $140,000.

All this around-the-clock negotiating freed up the money to agree to Leonard Armato's contract demands for Shaquille, who was signed on August 7. Armato was surprised that Orlando was able to clear the financial space to accomplish the deal, but he was impressed and he and Shaq really felt that they were wanted in Orlando. Ironically, after Shaq was signed, the Magic matched the offer sheet for Stanley Roberts, but traded him to the Los Angeles Clippers just before the season began. The big prize of all this, both figuratively and literally, was Shaquille.

Although Shaq was obviously thrilled to be signed to such a lucrative contract, he was also ready to work hard, and he went back to California to attend Pete Newell's Big Man camp. Pete Newell was a long-time college coach who was one of the most respected men in basketball. He had coached at the University of San Francisco, Michigan State University, and the University of California-Berkeley, winning the NCAA championship in 1959. He also was the U.S. Olympic coach in 1960 and was elected to the Basketball Hall of Fame in 1979. Although officially retired, Newell ran his camp every summer, almost exclusively for NBA players, and he improved their footwork, court awareness, shooting, ball handling, and defense. Newell said that Shaq was the best big man that he had seen at "this stage of his career." He worked hard and strived to improve for the entire two weeks of the camp.

Because of Leonard Armato's skills as an agent and Shaquille's obvious appeal, nationally, he had two large endorsement contracts (with Reebok and Pepsi) before he had played a minute in the NBA. The Reebok deal was for $10 million over five years, although it could be worth up to $20 million. Before the season began he had a five-year, $6 million contract with Spaulding Sporting Goods, which began advertising in January 1993 for Shaq basketballs, Shaq backboard and rim sets, and Shaq notebooks. He also had an exclusive trading card contract with Classic Trading Cards that brought him $2.5 million for two years. After the start of the season, there was a deal with a video distributor that would showcase Shaq's rapping talent, and another deal with Kenner Toys to make Shaq "action figures" soon followed. With his newfound wealth, Shaquille immediately took his mother to a Circuit City store. He wanted to have a new sound system for his home and all sorts of other gadgets like big screen TVs. He wanted cars and bought them. He wanted a new house for his parents and got that, as well as new cars for them. In his own words, he went through his first million in three days.

Because Shaq knew that there would be many people interested in getting money from him and because he also knew that he did not have the time nor the inclination to mange his money, he and Leonard Armato formed an investment firm to handle Shaq's finances. Shaq surrounded himself with people he knew that he could trust: his parents, Leonard, and longtime friends of his parents, mostly from Newark. These people constituted his managerial and security functions. One of those people was Dennis Tracey who was a friend of a man named Charles Giordano of Metaire, Louisiana. His wife, Dominque, earned her degree in fine arts from LSU just as Shaq was forming his company, and Tracey asked Dominique if she wanted to try designing a logo for Shaq's firm. Having seen him play many times at LSU, Dominique felt that she could capture what Shaq represented, and she designed a logo that had a globe spinning on a person's finger. Both Tracey and Shaq liked the design, and it appeared on the One-Al corporation business cards, envelopes, and stationery. Despite Shaq's new status, he maintained personal contacts with those with whom he'd grown up, as well as those who represented his time at LSU.

Cautionary observers of Shaq's new corporate status noted that his advertising success would be linked directly to how well he did as a player. These people noted that he had to have a good start as a player to have an impact for Shaq the advertiser. By mid-season, it was clear that advertisers who had pursued Shaquille had made good deals for themselves, as well as for him. Shaq had signed deals that would bring him at least $30 million over the next three to five years, in addition to his regular NBA playing contract. For the advertisers, he proved to be popular with both men and women of all age groups. As Leonard Armato observed, "He combines two things that are almost impossible to have together—incredible physical presence… and this tremendous likeability… which is very non-threatening to men and very endearing to women." Of course his age (20) and his baby face and big smile also made him very appealing to kids.

SHAQ DEBUTS IN THE NBA

Training camp for the Magic opened in October and soon after that the team was playing exhibition games against other NBA teams. On October 17, the Magic faced the Miami Heat in Shaq's NBA debut. Although it was still an exhibition game, Shaq's performance was impressive as he shot 11 of 16 from the floor and scored 25 points in the Magic victory. In the next two exhibition games against the Atlanta Hawks, Shaq had less of an impact, but through the six games that the Magic played, Shaq's performances impressed his coach, Matt Guokas, a former NBA player for 10 years with the 76ers, the Bulls, the Rockets, and the Kings and a former 76ers coach. He had expected Shaq to score 12 to 15 points per game, but upped his assessment to 20 to 25 as the real NBA season began.

The Magic opened the regular season on November 6, against the Miami Heat in the O-Dome, the Orlando home court. Nick Anderson scored 42 points to lead the Magic in scoring, but Shaquille had 18 rebounds to go with 12 points as the Magic won by a score of 110 to 100. Shaq fouled out of the game with 1 minute 32 seconds to go, but by that time, the result was not in doubt. He also brought the crowd to its feet near the end of the first quarter by snaring a defensive rebound, dribbling up court and exploding for a thunderous dunk just before time expired in the quarter. Shaquille assessed his play: "I think I played pretty well. I did commit a lot of silly fouls in the second half."

The Magic continued its winning ways through the next six games, losing only once, to Charlotte, whose rookie center, Alonzo Mourning, had still not signed a contract. In that game Shaquille had 35 points, but scored none in the fourth quarter as Charlotte won 112 to 108. The Magic then defeated the Washington Bullets by a 127 to 100 score as Shaq scored 31 points and grabbed 21 rebounds, but his teammates also were able to provide support as Nick Anderson scored 25, Dennis Scott 27; Scott Skiles, the point guard, got 12 rebounds. After the first week of the season, Shaq led the league in rebounding, with 16.4 per game, was fifth in scoring with 25.8, and was fourth in blocked shots with 3.4 per game. Admittedly, the season was not very far along, but Shaq had shown that he was going to be a force in the league, and the Magic was looking to make the playoffs for the first time in its history. On November 16, Shaq was the first NBA rookie named player of the week so early in his career (week two of the season). The Magic were in first place in the Atlantic Division as they headed to New York City and the legendary Madison Square Garden to meet Patrick Ewing and the New York Knicks. The Knicks had tied the Boston Celtics for the Atlantic Division title the year before, but had been defeated in seven games by Michael Jordan and the Chicago Bulls in the conference semifinals. Shaq had never played in the Garden, but had attended games with his dad when they had lived in Newark, so this appearance would truly be a dream come true for him.

The Magic traveled to New York in an unusual position, first place, as Shaquille, joined by Dennis Scott, Nick Anderson, and Scott Skiles were pacing the team with their scoring, rebounding, and overall play. Patrick Ewing was one of top centers in the history of the league and was in his eighth NBA season and had averaged more than 24 points per game for the previous three seasons. New York often drew well-known personalities to their games, but this crowd on November 21 also included Wilt Chamberlain, the player who Shaq was often compared to because of his size, strength, and scoring ability. Wilt had seen Shaquille play on television, but this would be the first time that he would see him in person. Wilt had been in the area for other reasons, and staying over a bit longer for this contest was too intriguing for him to pass up. The official seating capacity for the Garden is 19,763 for basketball, but more than 20,000 attended this game and they did not leave disappointed.

Shaquille entered the contest averaging nearly 27 points and 17 rebounds a game. He was held to 18 points, but still had 17 rebounds; Patrick Ewing had only 15 points and 9 rebounds. The Magic, however, scored only 77 points, 38 below the 115 that they were averaging before that game, and lost to the Knicks by a score of 92 to 77. The New York Knicks' coach, Pat Riley, double-teamed Shaq as soon as he received the ball with Patrick Ewing (7 feet, 240 pounds) and Charles Oakley (6'9", 245 pounds) or Charles Smith (6'11", 260 pounds), all of which was designed to wear Shaq down and convince him to give up the ball. The coverage led Shaq to commit seven turnovers. He also was forced to rush shots, which often came off his hand flat, rather than with the spin necessary for a good shot. Shaquille said after the game that he thought he did pretty well in scoring, rebounding, and blocking shots, but neither he nor his teammates' shots were falling (that is, they weren't making their usual percentage of shots), but he was not about to let one game worry him. Ewing was clearly impressed with Shaq, noting, "he's a great player. He plays hard and is very strong. He knows how to find people when he needs help in the post. He's going to be a great pro."

As for Wilt Chamberlain, he was also duly impressed with Shaquille, although he found comparisons to him inappropriate. Wilt had met Shaq when he, Shaq, Bill Russell, Bill Walton, and Kareem Abdul-Jabbar had filmed a commercial together; and Wilt found Shaq to be a young man with class, style, and enthusiasm. Wilt said that Shaq was a very graceful player for his size and predicted that he would get better and better, but noted that he had to work on some inside offensive skills. A little five foot jumper would make him tremendous, felt Wilt, who said that he'd like to work with Shaq. Wilt also said that Shaq had "terrifying" power but that he would get worn down by guys banging against him all the time unless he didn't go inside all the time.

Wilt also didn't see any real reason to compare the two of them, other than the fact that they were both big, black men. Wilt argued that he shot many more jump shots than people seem to recall and that Shaq almost never shoots a jump shot. Because there is little videotape or film of Wilt's great years of playing when he averaged between 36 and 50 points per game for six straight seasons (including a game in 1962 when he scored 100 points) and between 24 and 27 rebounds per game for nine straight seasons, many of today's fans cannot understand the manner in which he played and dominated the floor. Shaq, too, dominates the game, but in a style contrasting with that of Wilt Chamberlain. "I see Shaquille as a man totally playing his own game of basketball. The bottom line for me is I'd like to see him given the chance to play basketball with his own athletic ability and style, let him be Shaquille O'Neal and not the new Wilt Chamberlain, or the new anyone else."[4] One very big difference between Wilt and Shaquille was that Wilt never fouled out of an NBA game (nor did he ever foul out of a college or high school game), and he played in 1,205 NBA contests. Shaquille fouled out of his first game.

Shaq's presence was having an impact in every town where Orlando played. Orlando games often had many empty seats wherever they visited, but now tickets were so scarce that they were being "scalped" for far above their face value. Fans came earlier to watch warm-ups and stayed late in the hopes of getting an autograph from Shaq as he headed to the team bus, always at ease with the fans and happy to communicate with them. Shaq was making the biggest impact any rookie had made in the NBA since the arrival of Michael Jordan in 1984. He wasn't altering the game like Wilt or Michael had, but he was affecting the fan interest and gaining the attention of the players and coaches in the league. Chuck Daly, the coach of the New Jersey Nets, said this, when asked about Shaq: "He's a monster."

The next game of interest was Shaquille and the Magic's game against Hakeem Olajuwon and the Houston Rockets on November 25 in Orlando. The Rockets came to town with a six-game winning streak, and there was great anticipation around the match-up of the two centers, but the keys to what was a Magic victory were Scott Skiles and Dennis Scott. They combined for 58 points, 30 for Skiles and 28 for Scott, as the Magic won by a score of 107 to 94. In the Shaq-Hakeem duel, it was a draw. Both played about the same length of time (41 or 42 minutes) and were not encumbered by fouls (both had three). Olajuwon outscored Shaq 22 to 12, and they each had 13 rebounds. Hakeem had five blocks to Shaq's three, but the Rockets' center had five turnovers to Shaq's two. The most important statistic, however, was that the Magic won, and every player knew that was the only number that really mattered. The victory moved the Magic to six wins in nine games and they remained in first place in the Atlantic Division. The Magic then finished the month with two more victories to be eight and three, the best one-month record in the franchise's four-year history.

There was excitement wherever the Magic went, and Shaquille was at its center. Road attendance increased from 14, 949 to 17,270. A Reebok ad that featured Wilt Chamberlain, Bill Russell, Bill Walton, Willis Reed, and Kareem Abdul-Jabbar, along with Shaq; his dad, and legendary coach, John Wooden, was to be released by Reebok during the all-star game in February. The company was surprised and pleased by Shaquille's great success, but skeptics still remained within the marketing "community" as to whether Shaquille could have long-term success as a spokesperson for various companies. Some of these skeptics noted that basketball centers have rarely made it as big-time product endorsers. Others questioned whether he was likable enough to expand interest beyond basketball. There were some who said the big push would be at the end of the basketball season if Shaquille could somehow get his team into the playoffs.

Unfortunately the league began to "catch up" with the Magic, and they began a road trip that brought them disastrous results. The Magic was shooting 49.8 percent as a team and averaging 109.8 points a game, sixth in the league. Then the bottom dropped out. The Magic lost six in a row. These included road losses and home losses to the Celtics and Phoenix. Against Boston, Shaq had 26 points and 15 rebounds against Robert Parish, but the Celtics prevailed, 117 to 102. In Detroit, the Pistons won 108 to 103, with Dennis Scott topping Orlando with 38 points. Shaq had 17 points and 11 rebounds and was double or triple-teamed, but his teammates didn't shoot as well as they needed to win.

The loss to Phoenix at home, by a score of 108 to 107, came about as Shaquille went two for four on free throws in the last six seconds. He was hitting 54 percent from the line for the year, which hurt in close games, as teams chose to foul him rather than give him a chance to score. The Magic finally broke their losing with a decisive victory over Sacramento in Orlando, 112 to 91, as Shaq scored 22, had 20 rebounds, and blocked 7 shots. Orlando also shot well, once again, after the poor shooting during the losing streak.

During the streak, Shaq managed to find time to appear on the Arsenio Hall Show, singing with Fu Schnickens, his favorite rap group. Shaq drew good reviews and showed a national television audience that he was more than just a basketball player. Fans continued to follow him and the team, seeking to get autographs, to touch him, or just to talk to him. Shaq was being interviewed and featured in *Sports Illustrated* and the *New York Times Magazine*. People wanted to know what he did in his free time at home. He said that he liked to watch movies, mostly karate movies, and listen to music. At Thanksgiving he had a "Shaqsgiving Day" for homeless people in Orlando; he supplied tickets to kids for every Magic game and distributed toy-store gift certificates to children's homes for Christmas. Clearly Shaq was making an impact in the NBA, as well as in the Orlando community.

As the end of the year approached, the Magic were 9 and 9, disappointing after their fast start, but significantly improved over the previous season when they won their eighth game in late January on the way to a total of 21 wins. By the end of the year, the Magic were 13 and 11, and the Orlando fans were beginning to envision a spot in the playoffs for their team for the first time. The Magic closed the month with wins in five of their last seven games. Shaquille returned to his prior scoring heights, after being held to less than 20 points in a number of contests. He still was having foul trouble, however. In the December 22 game against the Utah Jazz, Shaq had 22 points in the third quarter, but picked up his fourth foul and was removed by Coach Guokas. When he was reinserted into the game with 10 minutes left in the contest, he scored six points, snared six rebounds and blocked three shots to spark the Magic to a 101 to 98 win. He finished with 28 points, 19 rebounds, and 5 blocks for the game. His 5 blocks gave him 87 for the year, a new Orlando record, with 60 games still remaining in the regular season. A week later Shaq failed to block a shot in a game for the first time in his brief NBA career. He did score 23 points and get 23 rebounds, but the Lakers edged the Magic in Orlando, 96 to 93.

As the season moved into January, there were concerns about whether Shaquille and the Magic could continue to play so well. For Shaq, the concern centered on the fact that the Magic was nearing the number of games a college team normally plays in a season, which was about 30. The fear was that Shaq (and other rookies) would start to wear down because they had never played so many games in such a short span, not to mention the much rougher competition. At about this time, the balloting for the NBA all-star game, to be played in February, was also taking place. Besides Shaq's impressive statistics, he also had great charisma and popularity, although his NBA career was only a couple of months old. As the polling continued through January, Shaquille led the veteran, Patrick Ewing, at the center spot for the Eastern Conference.

The Magic began 1993 with two close losses, dropping them to .500. Then they faced the Knicks for the second time in the season, but this time the game was in Orlando. In his second match-up with Patrick Ewing, Shaquille played the Knicks center to a draw. Shaq had 22 points and 13 rebounds to Ewing's 21 points and 12 rebounds, but the most noteworthy outcome was the Magic's victory by a score of 95 to 94. Later that week, fan balloting indicated that Shaquille was winning the battle for the starting berth in the all-star game. Shaq had almost 191,000 votes to nearly 98,000 for Ewing. This vote, along with the loss by the Knicks to the Magic, aroused the anger of the Knicks' coach, Pat Riley. He would be even angrier in February when the voting results were announced and

Shaquille had more than 825,000 votes to Patrick Ewing's just under 580,000. Clearly, it wasn't close and Riley was angry over the results as well as the process, whereby the most popular big man was elected, not necessarily the player performing the best. Shaquille had captivated the nation's fans with his play, his manner, and his enthusiasm. Patrick Ewing was not nearly as well liked. He was much more aloof, did not visit the fans and give autographs, and was not the personality that Shaquille was. He was highly respected by players and coaches in the league, but was hurt in all-star balloting by a large "anti-New York" vote among fans that was often present in the rest of the country.

Before this election was finalized, there was still a lot of basketball to be played. After the defeat of the Knicks, the Magic dropped two in a row at home to Indiana and Chicago. They then went on a three-game road trip, starting with games in Boston and Chicago. The outcomes seemed unfortunate for Orlando, but Shaquille and his teammates rose to the occasion. First, they knocked off the Celtics in a surprisingly easy victory, 113–94. Shaquille and Scott Skiles combined for 45 points (23 for Skiles, 22 for Shaq), Shaq also had 12 rebounds and 4 blocks, and Skiles had 15 assists as the Magic won for the first time ever in the Boston Garden. The Magic immediately left for Chicago where they won again the next night over Michael Jordan and the Bulls in overtime, 128 to 124. This was a most heralded win since the Bulls were two-time defending NBA champions and were led by MVP Michael Jordan, who scored 64 points. The Magic were again led by Skiles (31 points and 10 assists) and Shaquille (29 points and 24 rebounds, 5 blocks) as the Magic got above the .500 mark, once again, at 16 and 15.

At this point, Shaquille was leading all NBA rookies in scoring with 22.7 per game, and the Magic ended the month with a record of 18 and 19. In February, Shaq and his team continued to improve and showed no indication of tiring from the long season. In early February, the Magic defeated the Los Angeles Lakers, 110-97, the first time that Orlando had ever won in the Forum of Los Angeles. Shaquille had 31 points and 14 rebounds to lead the Magic who shot well from the floor. The next day (February 4), the all-star starters were announced and Shaquille was named the Eastern Conference center along with forwards Larry Johnson of Charlotte, Scottie Pippen, of Chicago, and guards Isaiah Thomas of Detroit and Michael Jordan of Chicago. Jordan, who was the last rookie named to start in an all-star game in (1985), was the biggest vote-getter overall, with just over 1 million votes. Also that week, it was announced that Shaq had signed another big endorsement contract, this time with Pepsi, for five years.

On Sunday, February 7, NBC decided to have the featured Sunday afternoon game be the Magic at the Phoenix Suns. At that time, the major networks did not begin regular telecasts of the NBA until the first of January, so Shaquille had only been seen as a professional by those with cable access. Initially, the network had planned to carry the Boston-Golden State game, but Shaquille's great popularity and his selection as the starter in the All-Star game changed the NBC executives' minds. They were not sorry that they did. Early in the first quarter of the game, Shaquille grabbed a rebound and went back up immediately for a powerful dunk. As he hung on the rim, his weight tipped the entire basket structure forward and raised the back of it off the ground. "After he let go, the collapsible underpinning slowly began folding into a storage position. It was a surreal scene, like something out of a science fiction movie."[5] It took about 35 minutes for the maintenance staff to realize that O'Neal's weight had broken a piece of the support system, wheel that structure out, and replace it with a back-up basket structure. It was the talk of the basketball world for a few days and would increase interest in watching Shaquille play. The game had a viewer rating that was nearly 50 percent higher than the previous weeks. The network saw him as a clear "ratings draw."

As for the game, the Suns, led by Charles Barkley, who had 28 points and 19 rebounds, defeated the Magic, 121 to 105. Shaq, hampered by foul trouble, played only 29 minutes before fouling out with just over three minutes to play. He still managed to score 20 points, but only 5 rebounds. Barkley coaxed Shaq into four of the fouls and Charles said after the game, "It's going to take some time for him to learn the game of basketball."

The Magic split their next two games before traveling to Charlotte on February 11 to play the Hornets and their rookie center from Georgetown, Alonzo Mourning. He had not signed with the team until the season had started, causing him to miss four games in the contract dispute. Now Mourning was rounding into shape, and there was great anticipation as the two rookie centers, one, 7'1" and 305 pounds, the other, 6'10" and 244 pounds, who were drafted Numbers 1 and 2 in the draft, met for the first time. Like Shaq, Mourning had an immediate impact on his team and the NBA, and, like Shaq, he had already broken the team record for blocks in a season in just 19 games.

Early in the game, Shaq snared a rebound over Mourning and rocketed to the basket for a massive dunk. Near the end of the game, Mourning returned the favor, grabbing a rebound and dunking over Shaquille. In between the two battled at near even terms. Mourning had 29 points, 15 rebounds, and 4 blocks; Shaquille had 27 points, 14 rebounds, and 2 blocks. Most important, Charlotte won by a 116 to 107 score, its fifth win in six games. After the contest both players said that they enjoyed the battle and they expected to see Charlotte-Orlando as the rivalry of the 1990s.

The loss to Charlotte left Orlando at 15 wins and 16 losses and Shaquille with averages for the year of 23.7 points, 14 rebounds, and 3.7 blocks per game. Still, Orlando Coach Matt Guokas felt that Shaq was being mistreated by the officials and complained to the league office. In one game Shaquille had scored 38 points, took down 16 rebounds, and blocked 8 shots but was called for nine turnovers, mostly traveling, that is, taking too many steps with the ball. Shaq said that he should have and could have had 50 points in the game, if not for the calls, which he said came after he was pushed. This was a familiar story for Shaq who had turned professional a year earlier because of his annoyance at being hammered so much in college games. One way to offset the pounding was to hit his free throws, but Shaquille was averaging only 54 percent on them and the fouling was bound to continue.

A week before the all-star game, the Knicks, with a seven-game winning streak, came to Orlando for the third meeting of the year between the Magic and the Knicks. This was shortly after O'Neal's selection over Ewing as starting center had been announced, and Patrick was determined to best his rookie counterpart. The game went to three overtimes before the Magic won by a score of 102 to 100. Shaquille got in foul trouble early and missed 16 of the 24 minutes in the first half, but it was Ewing who fouled out near the end of the first overtime. He finished with 34 points, 14 rebounds, and 4 blocks; Shaquille had 21 points, 19 rebounds, and 9 blocked shots (a new Magic record), with 6 of them in overtime. Shaquille shot horribly, hitting 3 of 17 in regulation and finishing with 8 of 25 from the floor, but he was pleased that his team had won. "That's what it's all about," he said.

The Magic were back at .500 and stayed that way as they split the final two contests before the all-star game. In Detroit, Shaq scored 46 points, but his 8 of 16 free-throw shooting, including four misses in overtime, were a key to the loss to the Pistons. After beating Denver at home, the Magic were positioned to make the playoffs, but the season was just half over. Shaquille headed to Salt Lake City for the all-star game weekend.

THE ALL-STAR GAME AND THE REST OF THE 1992–1993 SEASON

The NBA All-Star game had become a full weekend of entertainment by 1993, with a dunk contest and a three-point shooting contest, as well as an extended media day. This last event was mandatory, and when three players—Michael Jordan, Scottie Pippen, and B. J. Armstrong—all Chicago Bulls, missed the media session, they were each fined by NBA Commissioner David Stern. By contrast a number of stars, including Shaq, David Robinson, Isaiah Thomas, Charles Barkley, and Patrick Ewing, stayed beyond the prescribed time, answering questions and joking with reporters.

Some of the media noted that Shaq was the center of attention and curiosity among the players, as well as the fans. Some had not played against him yet, and most had seen him only once or twice and were interested in how he'd do in this type of game. Asked about who they wanted to see, most replied Shaq, if anyone. This group of respondents included Dominque Wilkins (nicknamed "the human highlight film" because of his many moves and dunks); Harold Miner, one of the slam-dunk contestants; future Hall of Famer Karl Malone, and all-star starter, Larry Johnson. Most of those questioned found Shaq to be a good guy and a nice person, and Shaq was low key about his presence. When asked about who people were coming to see, he responded with Michael Jordan or Charles Barkley. There was no doubting that he was going to be closely watched when the ball was tipped off on February 21.

Most all-star games are dominated by scoring, and this one was no exception. The final score was West 135, East 132 in overtime. For the first three quarters, Shaquille and Patrick Ewing played for about an equal time. The East team was coached by Ewing's coach in New York, Pat Riley, and he had already said how he felt about Shaquille being named the starter rather than Patrick Ewing. In the fourth quarter Shaq played less than two minutes, but then played most of the overtime. That latter period was played with Ewing in a kind of "twin towers" setup. Shaquille did not touch the ball much. For the game, Shaq had 14 points and 7 rebounds while impressing his peers with his play and his unwillingness to criticize his coach. What he did say about his first all-star game was, "I had fun."

Shaq returned to the Magic after the game, ready to steel himself for a playoff run, but the team continued to hover at the .500 mark through February and March. Shaq continued to be among the league leaders in scoring, rebounds, and blocks. Shaq returned to New Jersey just before his 21st birthday when the Magic met the Nets. Before a number of his old friends and relatives, Shaq was held to 18 points and was outplayed by Derrick Coleman of the Nets, who scored 34 points, including a few dunks over Shaq, as the Nets won 116 to 97. The next night the Magic lost in Milwaukee, and Shaq was again held to 18 points, 6 below his average. The Nets returned home on Shaq's birthday and played the Clippers the next night. Shaq and the Magic played much better, as they won 112 to 95. Shaquille had 23 points and 15 rebounds and Nick Anderson had 36 points.

The Magic were now 28 and 27, above .500 once again, but by the end of the month of March, they had slipped to 33 and 34. One notable loss was in San Antonio, where Shaquille had attended high school and where his parents and siblings still lived. Shaq wanted to play well in front of his hometown friends and relatives, but the Spurs defeated the Magic, 96 to 93. It was not a good performance for Shaquille. Coming off an embarrassing loss to the Dallas Mavericks, who broke a 19-game losing streak to beat the Magic two nights before, Shaquille and his team were hurt by injuries and stupidity against San Antonio. Scott Skiles and Dennis Scott were both out with injuries. Shaquille had distributed more than 500 game tickets to old friends, but despite their presence, he lost his temper in the fourth quarter of a close game and was ejected after arguing about an offensive foul call. The Magic had lost five games in a row to drop to 29 and 33, and their playoff chances seemed to be slipping away.

The final game of their road trip was in Denver with Dikembe Mutombo, and Shaquille came back to score 22 points and grab 12 rebounds, but Nick Anderson with 32 and Donald Royal with 25 points provided the support to defeat Denver, 114 to 108. With the victory, the Magic moved to within one game of the eighth, and final, playoff berth in the Eastern Conference. Considering that in the previous year, the Magic had been 14 and 49 at the same point in the season, the improvement was extraordinary, but now the team wanted the playoffs. Coach Guokas acknowledged that Shaquille was the reason that they had 30 wins already, and he had been recognized as the rookie of the month for every month of the season. Now he had to maintain his gaudy statistics, which were 24 points and 12 rebounds per game since the mid-season all-star break for Orlando to even have a chance at post season play.

April started with three straight losses for the Magic, but then they won four of five. They were at 37 and 38 with seven games to play. Two more losses followed, but then they won three of four as they headed into their final game at home against Atlanta. If the Magic won and Indiana lost, Orlando would make the playoffs. Shaq scored 31 points and took down 18 rebounds (following a 25-rebound performance the previous game) to lead his team over the Hawks, 104 to 85. Then the team waited to see how Indiana would do against Miami. The Pacers won, 94–88, to eliminate the Magic, even though the two teams both had records of 41 and 41. In the NBA tiebreaker system, the record in head-to-head competition was the first tie-breaker. They had split four games. The next criterion was total points against the opposite team. Indiana had outscored Orlando by five points in their four games and earned the playoff spot. The season was over for Shaquille and the Magic.

If there was any consolation in the heart-breaking manner in which they were eliminated, it was that the Magic would be eligible for the NBA lottery, once again, and might be lucky enough to draft another top player like Shaquille. Every great team has had at least two top stars. In recent years, Michael Jordan and Scottie Pippen of the Bulls are a good example. Despite Michael's greatness, the Bulls never won an NBA championship until Pippen joined the Bulls in 1987, after which they won six NBA titles in the 1990s. Perhaps the Magic could be fortunate enough to get a high pick and to select another impact player.

As for impact, Shaquille had certainly made one in his first NBA season. He scored just over 23 points per game (eighth in the league), averaged 13.9 rebounds per game (second in the league), averaged 3.53 blocks per game (second) and shot 56 percent from the floor (fourth). He was the only player to be ranked in the top 10 in four statistical categories and easily won the rookie of the year award. Not so great was the fact that he led the league in turnovers (307) and was third in fouls (321).

NOTES

1. Sam Smith, "Magic Pulls Shot at O'Neal out of Lottery Hat," *Chicago Tribune*, May 18, 1992, 10.

2. "O'Neal Thrilled Magic Picked Him," *Chicago Tribune*, May 20, 1992, 3.

3. Ibid.

4. Scott Ostler, "The Big Dipper and the Shaq, a Truthful and Honest Chamberlain Compares Himself and Rookie O'Neal," *Los Angeles Times* December 13, 1992 1.

5. "No Mere Backboard Breaker, O'Neal Brings Down the Housing," *Los Angeles Times*, Sports Desk, February 8, 1993, 6.

Chapter 6

THE MAGIC CONTINUES,
THEN VANISHES

In May the annual draft lottery was held and the Magic were very fortunate to again gain the Number 1 pick, although they had the least likelihood of that happening. With that pick, at the draft in June, the Magic selected Chris Webber, a 6'9" forward who led his University of Michigan team to the NCAA finals two consecutive years before leaving school after his sophomore year. He was considered the best player in the draft and ultimately was selected rookie of the year in 1993–1994, but not for Orlando. The team's management felt that Shaquille needed a point guard who could shoot, pass, and, maybe, rebound, and Anfernee "Penny" Hardaway from the University of Memphis seemed to fit the bill. Considering Scott Skiles's injuries and his own observation that he was a guard with limited skills who played hard, getting Hardaway was a good choice. Rather than pass on Webber, the Magic, instead, drafted him, then traded him to Golden State in return for Hardaway (whom they had drafted as the Number 3 pick) and three future first-round draft picks in 1996, 1998, and 2000. The choice was not popular among a lot of people in Orlando, but in retrospect, it was a good decision.

In addition to adding Hardaway, the Magic had made a significant change on their coaching staff, moving head coach Matt Guokas to the position of vice-president of player development and promoting assistant coach, Brian Hill, to the head coach job. Hill had been an assistant for three years after holding a similar position for four years with the Atlanta Hawks. Before joining the Hawks, he had been an assistant coach for Lehigh, Montclair State, and Penn State. Hill had no prior experience as an NBA head coach and questions were raised about his appointment, but he knew the team personnel and the organization so the Magic management was comfortable with their choice. The Magic's chances for improvement in the Eastern Conference certainly improved when Michael Jordan announced his retirement from the three-time NBA champion Chicago Bulls. The East would be a much more competitive contest in 1993–1994.

During the summer, Shaq was very busy. Besides his regular workouts (which were shortened by a tour of the Far East and Australia for Nike), he and Leonard Armato laid out a schedule that involved him in many aspects of promotion, as well as exploring other interests that Shaq had previously wanted to pursue. One of the most unusual was acting. Shaq was always a showman so he was thrilled when William Friedkin wanted Shaq to appear in a new movie, *Blue Chips*. Friedkin had won an Oscar as best director for *The French Connection* (which also won as Best Picture) in 1972 and had also been nominated for Best Director in 1974 for *The Exorcist*. The writer on this picture was Ron Shelton who had written *Bull Durham* and *White Men Can't Jump,* two well-received and well-known sports movies. And the star of the picture was Nick Nolte, a veteran film actor with nearly 20 years of top roles in movies such as *North Dallas Forty, Down and Out in Beverly Hills*, and *Prince of Tides* (for which he was nominated for an academy award).

The story focused on Nolte as Coach Pete Bell who needed better players and a winning record or risk losing his job. He discovers Shaq in his role as Neon Bodeaux on the playgrounds of New Orleans, and he becomes Mr. Nolte's coaching salvation. The film also included a smaller role for Anfernee Hardaway, which allowed Shaq to get to know his new teammate in a more unusual atmosphere.

Shaq received positive reviews for his role by a number of critics. Janet Maslin, the well-known film reviewer for *The New York Times*, found Shaq's performance "genuinely appealing as the most honest of the new recruits." She also noted that if the emphasis in the film had not been always on Nick Nolte, "it might be hard to remember that Mr. O'Neal has a day job."[1] This was certainly high praise for any actor, but even more so for a young man in his film debut with no background in acting.

The filming was done in Hollywood in June, moved to Indianapolis for basketball filming in July, then to New Orleans for some lengthier shots of Shaq on outdoor courts and in the city. Shaq enjoyed the film-making and it was the beginning of one of his many off-season hobbies/professions.

Another of those sidelines was the continuation of his rap singing. In May he did a rap film video with his favorite group, Fu Schnickens, and he would continue this, both formally and informally, after he installed a recording studio in his Orlando home. Also in that home was an enormous collection of high-tech video arcade games costing more than $100,000. The little kid in Shaq was still very apparent, and he did nothing to deny or hide that. He readily admitted how much he liked toys, music, and having fun.

Unlike many other stars, Shaq was not a recluse. Besides his unpublicized appearances at Children's hospitals and homeless shelters, he enjoyed driving around Orlando in his tricked out autos and he has many of them. He got his haircut in a largely African American neighborhood and when word would quickly spread of his presence, kids would flock to the site to see, talk with, and touch Shaq. He loved to do this, as well as just stopping at a stoplight, lowering one of his tinted windows, and chatting with the occupants of the adjacent car. Life was fun for Shaq, but it did not quell his intense desire to make the playoffs and to win an NBA championship.

And with the hopes of great improvement in the Magic on his mind, Shaq came to training camp in the fall of 1993. The roster had changed a little, but certainly looked to be better. Besides the addition of Penny Hardaway, the Magic had a year of playing with Shaq under their belts and the team could only get better. And they did.

Because of Shaq, the Magic had become a popular team throughout the country and, as the NBA sought to expand its presence in Europe, the Magic were scheduled to play two exhibition games in London against the Atlanta Hawks. The teams split the two games, but Shaquille had some dunks and blocks that brought the two sellout crowds to their feet. He was becoming an internationally recognized player, second only to Michael Jordan in that regard.

The Magic began the regular season with three straight victories, and Shaq averaged 38 points per game in those contests. He scored 42 points against Miami, 36 against the 76ers (while holding 7'6" Shawn Bradley, their Number 1 draft pick to seven points), then 37 points against Indiana. The Charlotte Hornets and Alonzo Mourning stopped the Magic win streak by defeating them in Charlotte, 120 to 87. Shaq had early foul trouble and sat out much of the game, including all of the fourth quarter. He still had 19 points, but he shot poorly (6 of 15 from the floor and 7 of 15 free throws) and his team lost by a big margin.

Later in November, Shaquille returned to New Jersey, as the Magic met the Nets in East Rutherford, less than 10 miles from Newark. Despite a cold, Shaq achieved his first "triple double" by scoring 24 points, taking 28 rebounds, and blocking 15 shots (the last two were career highs) as the Magic won, 87 to 85. Three nights later, in a match-up of the Number1 draft picks from the previous two years, Shaquille and the Magic topped

Chris Webber and the Golden State Warriors by a score of 120 to 107. Shaquille had 28 points and got Webber into foul trouble, limiting his minutes. He managed to score 13 points and grab 10 rebounds. Penny Hardaway scored a pro career high of 23 points and had 8 rebounds. The Magic closed the month with a loss to the Baltimore Bullets in Baltimore, leaving Orlando with a record of six wins and five losses heading into December.

In early December 1993, Shaquille's cold became influenza or he was weakened enough by the cold to be susceptible to the flu. Nevertheless, he continued to play. In a victory over Portland, he was eight of eight from the field in the second half and scored 26 points, and Scott Skiles had 20 assists to lead the Magic to a win over Portland. Two nights later, the San Antonio Spurs and David Robinson were too powerful for the Magic, as the Spurs won their seventh straight, 94 to 84. Shaq had 21 points and 19 rebounds, but his teammates provided little help in this game. The Magic flew to Cleveland after the game and the next night they defeated the Cavaliers, 87 to 83, behind Shaquille's 23 points and 15 rebounds.

Shaquille had become not only the NBA's most recognized figure but its most marketable. Michael Jordan had retired after the 1993 season and was attempting to become a major league baseball player. The void left by his considerable absence was filled, at least in part, by Shaquille. He was leading the league in scoring with about 30 points per game, was the top field goal shooter, and was second in rebounds. In addition, Shaquille was now the most recognizable active NBA player. He was on the cover of *Gentlemen's Quarterly* in November with a story profiling his basketball, his life, and his corporate endorsements. He also was on the cover of an issue of *Rolling Stone* in December, only the second NBA player to appear there (Kareem Abdul Jabbar was the first). Shaq's new rap single, "I Got Skillz," and the album, "Shaq Diesel," were the reason for his appearance on the cover of a music magazine. The CD entered the Billboard chart at Number 11 in the last week of November, with most lyrics for the 12 songs written by Shaq.

In December, *Forbes* magazine published their annual list of the world's 40 highest-paid sports stars for 1993. Despite his retirement, Michael Jordan retained the top spot with $36 million with two boxers and two auto racers in the next four slots. Moving up quickly to Number 6 was Shaquille with $15.2 million, of which $3.3 million was basketball salary and the rest commercial endorsements.

Shaq's recognition as a commercial and musical icon was gratifying, as well as rewarding, to him, but his major concern was trying to win basketball games and get the Magic into the playoffs. He was also drawing more fans to the arenas of the NBA; in his first 100 NBA games, only four games in which he played were not sold out. A very encouraging game was the contest against the Detroit Pistons, a consistent playoff team in the past, now heading into a season of disappointment. Down 83–66 entering the fourth quarter, the Magic rallied behind Penny Hardaway to edge the Pistons, 91–89. Shaquille led the Magic with 27 points and 16 rebounds, but made only 7 of 19 from the free-throw line. Hardaway had 20 points. Three nights later Shaquille had 30 points, 12 rebounds, and 8 blocks to lead the Magic over the Boston Celtics by a 117 to 102 score. Scott Skiles had 24 points for the Magic. The rest of the team was supporting Shaquille with scoring and defense, and in mid-December, the Magic managed to beat Portland by 15 points, extending their lead as Shaquille sat on the bench for much of the second half with four fouls. Shaq still had 23 points, despite sitting out for more than 15 minutes.

Shaquille was also sitting for more than simple personal fouls. He was becoming more annoyed at the refereeing and the physical nature of the game. No one was going to sympathize much with a 7'1", 300 pound player, and that may have been why Shaquille felt bothered enough to retaliate. In his rookie year he had been fined $7,500 and suspended for a game (which cost him $36,585 in lost salary) for punching Alvin Robertson, then with the Pistons. In November 1993, he was fined $5,000 for making derogatory remarks about officiating. Then in mid-December he was charged with a flagrant foul and ejected for hammering Shawn Kemp of the Seattle Supersonics as he drove for the basket. The blow knocked Kemp into a television camera and resulted in a cut over his eye and a bruised knee. Shaquille was subsequently fined another $5,000. The money lost had little impact on Shaquille, but creating an appearance of hooliganism did. Shaq insisted that it was not a dirty foul and the momentum simply carried Kemp into the camera.

Shaq's concern about being seen as a thug was justified. He was also being characterized by some as a whiner, especially after a game against the Atlanta Hawks where Jeff Turner of the Magic was ejected for arguing a no-call against Shaquille. Shaq was also ejected after receiving two technical fouls for unleashing a string of obscenities at officials who had called a foul on him after failing to call fouls on players for doing, what he felt, was the same thing to him. Nevertheless, Shaq continued to lead the NBA in scoring, with 28.5 points a game. The Magic also had 10 wins in 17 games in December to have a record of 16 and 12, second to the New York Knickerbockers in the Atlantic Division. During December Shaquille had averaged 27.9 points per game and 14 rebounds a game, and he was named the NBA player of the month for December. He also had a career-high 49 points in one game, a loss in Indiana to the Pacers, 111 to 105.

The Magic faced those same Knicks on January 4 in Madison Square Garden, but John Starks and Patrick Ewing were too much on that night for Shaquille and the Magic. Starks had 39 points and Ewing had 26 points and grabbed 19 rebounds, as the Knicks won 100 to 95. Shaquille had 26 points, but was limited to just 5 rebounds because they boxed him out off the boards very well. If the Magic were to go to and advance in the playoffs, they were likely to face the Knicks, so this game was more than just another game. The Magic recovered from their loss to defeat the Bulls and the Bullets. In the latter game, Shaq not only had 29 points and 19 rebounds but had another flagrant foul called on him. This meant that with his next one, he would be suspended for a game. Shaq felt that he didn't deserve the flagrant call, but he vowed to be more careful while still playing in his usual aggressive manner. The Magic victory moved them to a record of 19 and 13, only three games behind the Knicks.

Shaq and the Magic then met the Houston Rockets, the team with the best record in the Western Conference. Houston had a four-game winning streak and the Magic, of course, had a modest two-game win skein. One team would have to end its streak, and that team turned out to be the Rockets, as they fell to the Magic, 115 to 100. Penny Hardaway had 28 points and 6 assists, and Shaquille had 28 points and 7 rebounds against Hakeem Olajuwon, who finished with 26 points and 11 rebounds. He was held to one point in the fourth quarter, a period in which Houston also had nine turnovers.

By mid-January, Shaquille was leading the NBA in scoring (28.3 points per game), was fourth in rebounding (12.6), second in field goal accuracy (61%), and seventh in blocks (2.88); and the Magic were a cinch, it seemed, not only to make the playoffs but to finish as one of the top teams in the conference. Shaq was still struggling with free-throw shooting. Against the 76ers in late January, he had 33 points in a Magic victory, but made only 3 of 13 free throws.

THE ALL-STAR GAME AND THE REST OF THE SEASON

On January 27, the starters for the All-Star game were announced and there was little debate about Shaquille being named a starter again, considering his great performance and that of the Magic so far in 1993–1994. Shaquille was the second highest voter-getter overall to Charles Barkley. The game would be played in late February.

The Magic ended a great month with another victory, this time over the Washington Bullets by a score of 103–99 before a sellout crowd of almost 19,000 in Landover, Maryland. Shaq had 27 points, but his 3 of 10 free-throw shooting kept the game close. Still, with the victory the Magic were 26 and 17 and barely behind the Knicks.

That weekend, the Super Bowl was held and Reebok debuted a new ad featuring Shaquille singing his rap song, "Shoot Pass Slam." Other commercials featuring O'Neal were being criticized for the messages that they were sending. Harvey Araton, a respected sportswriter from the *New York Times,* complained about a Pepsi commercial, a Reebok commercial, and an ad for long distance service. In the first one Shaquille bent a rim, in the shoe spot he smashed a basketball backboard with a dunk, and in the phone spot his father slammed a receiver down, causing the phone booth glass to shatter. Both Araton and NBA officials decried these ads, which sent a message of destruction of property as acceptable to television viewers. Leonard Amato defended the ads and the way Shaq was being "packaged," but Araton had a lot of support in his efforts to remove this type of "gratuitous" violence from commercials.[2]

The 1994 All-Star game was played in Minneapolis on February 13. Despite the lack of controversy over Shaquille being voted a starter, his performance in this game was not up to his work in the NBA up to that point. Shaq didn't make a shot until the third quarter of the game and didn't have a dunk until the final minute of the contest, which the East won easily, 127 to 118. Shaq finished with 2 of 12 from the field, as well as 4 of 11 from the free-throw line for a total of eight points. Unlike most All-Star games, Shaq was double teamed by the West players from the start, and he was unable to get to the basket very often, much less have an open shot. He was philosophical about this and claimed to take none of it personally. It was clear, however, that he would respond by playing even more aggressively for the rest of the season, pushing the Magic into the playoffs.

One reason for some resentment on the part of certain players might have been that *Blue Chips,* the movie that Shaq and Penny had filmed in the summer, was released at All-Star time. The reviews of the movie were mixed, ranging from predictable and slow to great family entertainment. Despite the uneven reviews, almost all the reviewers praised Shaq's acting, although one noted, jokingly, that Shaq had a "promising future in movies as long as he continues to play huge basketball players."

After the All-Star game, the Magic got a big boost from the schedule that had them playing seven home games in a row. At the same time, the players were getting better at meshing as a unit. Shaquille and Penny formed a great combination of inside strength and outside shooting or driving. Dennis Scott, Shaquille's best friend on the team, was deadly as a shooter when he was healthy. Scott Skiles could replace Penny as the point guard as Hardaway shifted to the shooting guard spot. Nick Anderson was a deadly shooter and quick defender. The rebounding was still a bit too reliant on Shaquille, but the team found a rhythm that led them to a franchise-record seven victories in a row. The streak started at home but included away games also. The last victory was against Charlotte, which was heading in the opposite direction, having lost five in a row, jeopardizing their opportunity to make the playoffs. This game was at the end of February, and the Eastern Standings at that time showed that the Magic were in second place, only two games behind the Knicks in the Atlantic Division. In the overall Eastern Conference standings, they were in fourth place, also behind Atlanta and Chicago. Shaquille had injured his knee during the winning streak, but he kept playing. His game was slowed a bit, but even playing at 85 or 90 percent his best, Shaquille was a dominant force. The fear was that he might risk further injury, but the physicians involved felt that would not be the case.

The release of *Blue Chips*, "Shaq Diesel," the many commercial endorsements, and an autobiography (written with Jack McCallum of *Sports Illustrated*) and the ascension of the Magic to great success caused a number of basketball observers to predict that Shaq was overcommitted and would "burn out" soon. Many saw these other things as distractions that would affect Shaq's basketball play. Still, the criticism was difficult to take when Shaq continued to lead the league in scoring (28.7 points per game) and was in the top five in rebounding (12.5 rebounds per game). The Magic's coach, Brian Hill, defended his star center, noting that "he works as hard as anyone and has expanded his game."[3] Hill also noted that the addition of a player who could "do the dirty work,", that is, rebound, play strong post-up defense, and set bone-shattering picks, would be a big help to Shaquille and the Magic. Of interest, these same critics also saw Orlando as being a championship caliber team for at least the next four or five years because of Shaq and Penny.

The Houston Rockets ended the Magic's seven-game win streak in Houston on March 1, as Hakeem Olajuwon (26 points) outplayed Shaq (19 points on 8 of 19 shooting). A few days later the San Antonio Spurs defeated Orlando by a 111 to 103 score. This was a doubling bitter defeat for Shaq, as he lost before his friends in San Antonio and because he was outplayed by David Robinson, with whom Shaq was battling for the league scoring championship. Entering the game, Shaq was averaging 28.8 and Robinson 28.7 points per game. Robinson scored 36 points and had 13 rebounds before the crowd of 34,325 and a national television audience; Shaq had 32 points and had 11 rebounds.

Late in March, the last two players for the so-called Dream Team II squad were to be named. The first dream team in 1992 was the first group of NBA players to represent the United States in Olympic basketball, and they smashed all comers in winning the gold medal in Barcelona, Spain. That team included Michael Jordan, Magic Johnson, Larry Bird, Charles Barkley, and Patrick Ewing. Now a second "dream team" was being entered into the world basketball championships to be held in the summer of 1994. The idea was that this team would stay together in off-seasons and prepare for the 1996 Olympics in Atlanta. There were two spots open on the team, and Shaq was an obvious choice, but there were problems because of endorsements. Coca-Cola was one of the sponsors of the world championships and, for that reason, Shaq, who endorsed Pepsi, would not play for the team and dropped off the squad in October. In meetings with the NBA, Shaq's representatives, and those of Pepsi held in March, Pepsi agreed to allow Shaq to play without any negative effect on their relationship. A *Wall Street Journal* story noted that Shaq was now Number 2 in endorsement income, second only to the recently retired Michael Jordan.

Still, this good news was offset by the continuing mediocre play of the Magic in March. The Knicks ran off a 13-game winning streak, and the Magic fell eight games behind by the end of the month, barely ahead of Cleveland for the Number 5 seed in the East. Shaq had also fallen to a tie for second in league scoring, despite upping his average to 29 points per game. He was second in rebounding (13.0 rebounds per game) and shooting percentage (60.3%) and fifth in blocks (2.88 per game).

In April, Shaq and the Magic went nine and six to finish with 50 wins and 32 losses, by far the best record in Orlando's young history. They finished seven games in back of New York in the Atlantic Division and the Number 4 seed in the Eastern Conference. Without Michael Jordan, the Bulls still finished with 55 wins, but there were no heavy favorites for the NBA Playoff Championship. Seattle had won 63 games and Houston, 58, which were the most of any team, but six other teams had won at least 50 games so the race for the top seemed wide open.

Shaq ended the year second in scoring with an average of 29.3 to David Robinson's 29.8. He was second in rebounding with 13.2 per game to Dennis Rodman's 17.3. and led the league in shooting percentage at 59.9 percent. Shaquille also finished sixth in blocks with 2.88 per game. He did not finish in the top 10 in turnovers, although both Hakeem Olajuwon and Patrick Ewing did. Shaq was mentioned by some as a possible most valuable player candidate, but the favorites were Shawn Kemp of Seattle,

Hakeem Olajuwon, and David Robinson. The last two were picked on the first and second All-Star teams with Shaq on the third team at center.

The Magic began the playoffs against Indiana and were swept by the Pacers in three games, two of them in Orlando and decided by a total of three points. All of a sudden the season was over for Shaq and the Magic, and they were forced to watch the playoffs from the stands or at home as Houston, behind eventual MVP Hakeem Olajuwon, defeated the New York Knicks in seven games in the finals to claim the title.

NOTES

1. Janet Maslin, "Of Dunkers and Dollars," Review of *Blue Chips*, *New York Times*, February 18, 1994, C3.

2. Harvey Araton, "Shattering O'Neal's Slamfest," *New York Times*, January 5, 1994, B7.

3. Alan Truex, "He's a Magic Man/Shaq Potion Potent, but May Not Last," *Houston Chronicle*, March 1, 1994, 1.

A frisky, young Shaquille with his first team, the Orlando Magic. Courtesy of Photofest.

Shaq prepares to go up for a power move against Desagana Diop of Dallas in Game One of the 2006 Finals. AP Photo/David J. Phillip.

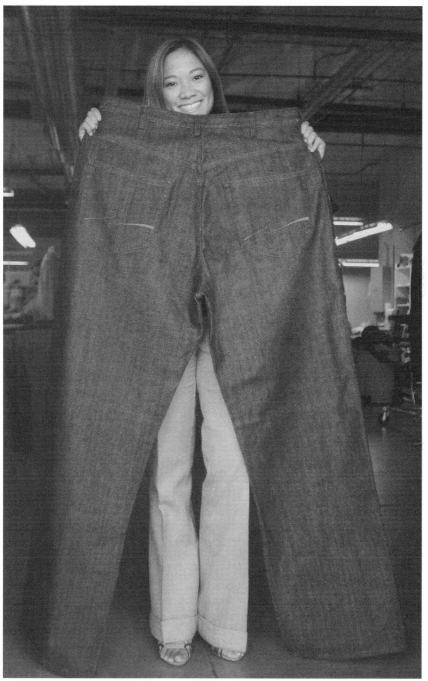

Here is some idea of how big Shaquille really is. Lead designer Jhoanna Wiegman holds up a pair of custom jeans made for Shaquille O'Neil at Elevee Fine Clothing in Van Nuys, California, on December 5, 2005. © Ann Johansson/Corbis.

Lakers O'Neal hugs mother after receiving a degree from LSU on December 15, 2000, eight years after he finished his playing career at LSU. © Reuters/Corbis.

Chapter 7

PREPARING FOR A NEW SEASON: THE WORLD CHAMPIONSHIPS

The summer of 1994 was more basketball-focused for Shaquille than his previous summer of moviemaking, recording, and commercial ventures. He returned to LSU early in the summer to take business courses toward his graduation. There were no movies and no rap albums. Instead, the World Championship of Basketball, under the supervision of FIBA (the Federation of International Basketball Associations), was to be held in Ontario, Canada in August. This tournament, which had begun in Buenos Aires, Argentina in 1950, had not been totally successful for the United States, as they had won two gold, three silver, and two bronze medals in the years it had competed. The United States had been dominant in Olympic basketball from the introduction of the sport in 1936 until 1972 when the U.S. team was upset in a famous loss at the last second by the Soviet Union team in Munich, Germany. After that loss, the United States won again in 1976 and 1984, but finished third in 1988. FIBA then allowed NBA players to compete for the United States and the 1992 dream team came about.

The 1994 U.S. team in Toronto was intended to stay together through the 1996 Olympics in Atlanta. As noted earlier, Shaquille had been named to the team, but a sponsorship dispute forced him to resign, only to be added a few months later after the dispute was resolved. With that dispute behind them, the team practiced together for less than two weeks before playing exhibition games to "tune up" for the World Championship Tournament. It was anticipated that Russia (the former Soviet Union), Yugoslavia, and Brazil would be the toughest foes for the United States, as all had beaten the U.S. team in World Championship competition in the past.

The tournament was to be played with 16 teams, in pools of four at two sites in Ontario, Canada. Exhibitions were scheduled for late July, with the

United States meeting Germany in Charlotte, North Carolina, and then playing July 31 in Oakland, California against the U.S. Goodwill Games team, made up of top college players. In the first game, Shaquille was seen as the most intimidating factor in the 114–81 U.S. victory. Shaq had thunderous dunks and bulled his way to the basket for 14 points. In the next game he had 18 points and 8 rebounds in less than 20 minutes of action. He looked ready for the tournament, and the U.S. coach, Don Nelson of the Golden State Warriors, called Shaq, "the best big man in the world."

The opening games seemed to confirm Nelson's assessment and the domination of the U.S. team. Shaq was seen as the Number 1 attraction for the tournament, both on and off the court. He was often seen in various places around Toronto, but he was never missed on the court. In the first three games, all easy U.S. victories, Shaquille averaged more than 20 points per game, shot 75 percent from the floor, and was best in the tougher games. Against Brazil he had 27 points in a 105 to 82 victory, capping that performance with a last second explosive dunk after Joe Dumars stole the ball and passed to a wide-open Shaq.

In the quarter-final rounds, Shaq and the United States continued their onslaught. They swamped Australia by 50 points, then defeated Russia, 111–94. Shaquille had 21 points on 10 of 11 shooting from the floor. This victory moved the United States into the semifinals to face Greece.

In an effort to slow down the U.S. squad, Greece kept two players in the backcourt on offense for most of the game and packed the inside on defense to force the U.S. team to shoot three-point shots, which they did, 45 times. The U.S. team shot only 40 percent, after shooting 60 percent for the first five games, but still won 97 to 58. Shaq was bottled up on offense by the double and triple teaming, but still snared 16 rebounds. Russia upset undefeated Croatia, 66 to 64, to make the championship game less exciting. The result was an easy U.S. victory over a tired Russian team. The score was 137 to 91, with Shaq getting 18 points, which was his average for the tournament. His dominance was clear to all as he was voted the tournament's most valuable player. It was the second gold medal and MVP for Shaq in international competition, and he looked forward to the 1996 Atlanta Olympics to make it three of each. Meanwhile, however, there was an NBA season to play.

THE 1994–1995 SEASON

It was clear to Shaq, as well as to Coach Brian Hill, that the Magic needed a big forward to push the team further in the playoffs in 1994–1995. General Manager Pat Williams couldn't rely on the draft lottery to get such a player because Orlando had finished so high in 1994. Instead, he pursued a free agent, Horace Grant, one of the cornerstones of the Bulls' three championships and a veteran of seven NBA seasons. In 1993–1994 he had his best scoring (15 per game) and rebounding (11 per game) and was a perfect complement to the Magic players. Shaquille pushed for the Magic to pursue him and he told Grant how much he hoped he'd consider playing with Orlando. Shaquille had to be careful not to do anything that could be construed as tampering with a player still under contract to another team. Ultimately, the Magic did sign Grant, although there was controversy surrounding that signing. Nevertheless, the Magic now had a powerful veteran forward to complement the inside game of Shaq and the ball handling of Penny Hardaway. The Magic also signed veteran guard Brian Shaw. Great things were anticipated in Orlando.

The preseason training camp opened without Penny Hardaway, who was holding out for a significant increase in his contract. He signed after 10 days of camp for a contract worth only slightly less than Shaq was to make in 1994–1995. Rather than gripe or try to renegotiate, Shaquille supported Hardaway in his efforts and was happy to get him back in camp. Some critics thought that Hardaway's high salary after only one season might hurt team morale, but that wasn't the case. Nick Anderson was very supportive of Penny, and Shaq said the size of Hardaway's contract was fine with him. He was not, he said, a jealous person. What was a problem was that many Orlando fans were upset, because these big salary increases would be offset by large increases in ticket prices. Many fans booed Hardaway when he took the floor in Orlando for the team's fourth exhibition game, but Penny did not seem bothered by that.

The media had installed Orlando as one of the favorites to win the Eastern Conference, along with New York, Indiana, and Charlotte. Shaquille' summer basketball in Canada and his regular workouts made him appear stronger and sleeker, according to many of the basketball writers who followed the team. Brian Hill agreed, noting that he appeared bigger in the chest, although still in great shape. The hope was that he'd improve his 55 percent shooting from the free-throw line that had made him a liability of sorts at the end of close games. Teams fouled him in close games to put him on the line, thinking that their odds were better at catching the Magic in this manner.

One unexpected highlight at the end of the Magic training camp was the naming of Shaquille as the recipient of the USA Basketball Male Athlete of the Year award. This was based largely on Shaquille's performance for the U.S. team in the World Championships, as well as his great NBA season. Shaq accepted the award with grace and humility, thanking his teammates for all their support on the Magic and the World Championship squad.

The Magic ended the exhibition season with six wins in eight games, but that would mean nothing as the team began the "real" season in early November. Shaquille seemed fine after missing some early practices with a dislocated big toe, and new starter Horace Grant was recovered from a pulled groin muscle. The first week of the season was good for both Shaq and the Magic. The team defeated Philadelphia easily and edged the Charlotte Hornets, 130 to 128. In the first game, Shaq had 30 points and 9 rebounds. In the second, he had 46 points and 20 rebounds.

The first month of the season was very similar to the exhibition season. The Magic burst out to early leads and won 10 of the first 12 games. By December 1, they had a three-game lead in the Atlantic Division and in the Eastern Conference. Shaquille was leading the league in scoring with just over 31 points per game and was averaging 12 rebounds a game. He also produced his biggest numbers when the games were on the line. The third game of the season, in Madison Square Garden, had the atmosphere of a playoff game and Shaquille came up with 41 points and 17 rebounds, but the Magic lost 101 to 99 to Ewing and the Knicks. Three weeks later that loss was avenged in Orlando as the Magic routed the New Yorkers, 125 to 100; Shaquille scored 38 points, leading the Magic to their ninth straight triumph. They hadn't lost since the game in New York.

In between those games against the Knicks, the Magic faced Houston, the defending NBA champions and their star, Hakeem Olajuwon, in the O-Dome. The score was Orlando 117 to Houston 94, with Shaq scoring 30, Penny 29, and Nick Anderson, 25. The Magic outrebounded Houston, 53 to 37, as Horace Grant kept Olajuwon off the boards, although Hakeem still had 27 points. The Magic had shown that they were a team that could play with any team in the league, and they were determined to advance in the playoffs in the Spring, perhaps to an NBA title.

At about this time, Shaq's second rap album, "Shaq Fu: da Return," was released as was his first video game, Shaq Fu. Rather than a basketball game, this was a martial arts adventure. The reviews were good for both and the "Shaq commercial machine" moved on.

In December, Shaq and his teammates continued their dominating play. After losing to Atlanta to end their winning streak, they won 12 of their next 15 games to end December with a record of 23 wins and only 6 losses.

The Magic had the best record in the league as 1994 ended, and they were getting recognition as the class of the Eastern Conference and one of the favorites to reach the NBA finals. Shaquille and Penny were also seen as tops at their positions. A number of writers were now touting Shaq as the league's MVP. He continued to improve his game, adding low post moves such as a baby hook and a turnaround jump shot, and Coach Hill echoed his previous statements regarding how hard Shaq worked. Critics of Shaq had emerged in the previous season saying he didn't have a range of shots and couldn't shoot free throws, pass out of the double team, or win a playoff game. Now writers were noticing his improvements in the first three areas.

In a lucky scheduling match-up, the Magic and the Phoenix Suns were slated for a nationally televised game in Arizona on January 22, 1995. The two teams had the best records in the NBA, Orlando being 30 and 7 and Phoenix 29 and 8. In addition the Suns had a very popular star, Charles Barkley, to match Shaquille in fan appeal. The game was being touted as a possible preview of the NBA finals. The game was equal to the hype, as the Suns edged the Magic in overtime by a score of 111–110. Shaq had 24 points but missed three close shots in overtime to keep Phoenix close enough to win. The victory left the two teams tied for the NBA's best record.

At the end of January the all-star balloting for the February 12 game in Phoenix was announced. For the third year in a row, Shaquille was named the starting center for the Eastern Conference, and he was to be joined by Penny Hardaway in the starting lineup. Shaq's 29.5 points per game still led the league and Penny was averaging 21.4 with 6.6 assists per game. Shaq was also slated to sing as part of the all-star game entertainment. He would be joined by a number of other performers, but his presence as a player and performer was certainly unique. Because the Magic had the best record in the Eastern Conference, Brian Hill, their coach, would also coach the Eastern Conference squad against Paul Westphal, the Phoenix Suns' coach.

The All-Star game was in two more weeks, but there was lots of basketball to be played before the season ended as the Magic set their sights on a championship. In a mishap at his home, Shaq stepped on a piece of broken glass in the kitchen, causing a one-inch cut that needed to be surgically closed. He was forced to miss a game, but the Magic still defeated the Bucks. The victory left the Magic with a record of 35 wins and 8 losses, 7 games ahead of the Knicks in the Atlantic Division and 8 1/2 games ahead of both Charlotte and Cleveland, the leaders of the Central Division of the Eastern Conference.

In the first week in February, the Magic lost two games in a row for the first time all season. The only team to still not have lost two games in a row was the Phoenix Suns and with the Magic loss, the Suns now had the best record in the league. This would be important in the playoffs where the team with the best record would have the home court advantage in each series played. The Magic lost to Indiana by 12 points in Indianapolis. The Pacers had swept the Magic in the playoffs the previous spring, so Orlando needed to overcome this psychological edge next time the teams played. This game was played without either Horace Grant or Nick Anderson, both out with injuries, and Anfernee (Penny) Hardaway was cut above the eyebrow in the third quarter, missing six minutes while he received two stitches. Shaquille had 20 points and 10 rebounds, both below his average, and the Pacers' center, Rik Smits, had 27 points and 10 rebounds. It was clear that Shaquille would need the help of his injured teammates to get the Magic into the playoffs at top seed.

SHAQ'S ALL-STAR GAME

The All-Star Game in Phoenix felt, to many, like the Shaquille O'Neal show. Shaq was rapping at the MTV jam and, again, at the game. A popular single off his new album was "Biological Didn't Bother," which was dedicated to Phil Harrison for being the father that Joe Toney never tried to be. His Reebok commercial, featuring a team of Shaqs playing another team of Shaqs, was wildly popular. And of course, Shaq was the best player on what was seen as the best team in the league. All-Star breaks are often the time to consider what has happened thus far in a season and predict the remainder of the year. Judging by the large number and diversity of the fans and reporters, Shaq was the story of the season. Reporters from Japan, Germany, and Italy sought his comments, as did the American journalists. Shaq's agent, Leonard Armato, commented on a question about Shaquille's popularity. "Shaq is appealing," he said, "because of a combination of strength and sensitivity that doesn't exist in the world.... That's what a lot of the advertising and marketing has tried to bring out." A Reebok spokesman, Dave Fogelson, recalled Shaq putting on a dunking show in Greece in September, then passing out souvenirs. He also remembered going into a London toy store on the same trip, posing for pictures, signing autographs, and making people leave happy.

The all-star game, itself, is more of an offensive display than a defensive, playoff exhibition. Shaq scored 22 points on 9 of 16 shooting and took 7 rebounds in 26 minutes of play to lead the East but the West destroyed the East, 139 to 112 and Mitch Richmond of the Warriors, who had 23 points for the West took the MVP. The more important MVP, that of the league for the season, was discussed a lot at the game and three candidates, all centers, were again seen as the front runners. Hakeem,

Shaq, and David Robinson were also the top three scorers in the league and were among the leaders in rebounds and blocks. With their respective teams all in contention for division championships, the MVP vote would likely be decided by the successes of their teams.

The biggest story of March in the NBA was the return of Michael Jordan. After retiring to play professional baseball and missing all of the 1993–1994 season and most of the current season, Jordan returned, hoping to lead the Bulls to a title, once again. The Magic played the two months of the season as barely a .500 team, going 15 and 12 to finish with 57 wins, good enough to win the Atlantic Division and the Eastern Conference title, but not as good as San Antonio, Utah, or Phoenix, all of whom had 59 wins or more. Still the Magic would have the home court advantage (where they'd lost only 2 of 41 games) throughout the Eastern playoffs. Individually, Shaquille led the league in scoring, with 29.3 points per game. Hakeem had 27.8 and David Robinson 27.6. Shaq finished third in rebounds with 11.4 per game, second in field goal percentage, and sixth in blocks. He also led the league in free throws attempted, but his 53 percent shooting from the league continued to plague him and might hurt him in MVP voting, which was taken at the end of the season and before the playoffs began.

THE 1994–1995 PLAYOFFS

Sixteen teams make the playoffs and the Magic, as the Number 1 seed in the East, would play the Celtics in a five-game opening series. Although the Celtics had finished as the Number 8 seed, the recent difficulties that Shaquille had had with them, as well as the fact that the Magic had lost their last seven games in a row on the road, made the series outcome more uncertain. The first two games were in Orlando, but the Celtics managed to hand Orlando its third home loss of the season as the teams split the two games. Shaquille did not shoot well from the field, but he did cause the "hack-a-Shaq" defense to go awry by hitting 11 of 14 from the free-throw line. He had 23 points in 27 minutes in an annihilation of the Celtics, 124 to 77. Then Boston managed to bounce back and win two nights later, 99 to 92.

Despite the home loss, the Magic and Shaq went to Boston and topped the Celtics in two straight contests to end their road-losing streak and eliminate the Celtics. Shaq had 20 points and a season-high 21 rebounds in the 82 to 77 victory. Then the Magic ended the series with a 95 to 92 victory as Shaq had 25 points and 13 rebounds. Horace Grant had 23 points and 10 rebounds to support Shaq in scoring and on the boards.

After being swept the year before in their first series as a franchise, there was pleasure in the first-round victory, but there was also wariness. The next opponent for the Magic would be the Chicago Bulls, with Michael Jordan. Although he was still not in great basketball shape, Jordan had still averaged 27 points per game in 17 contests, and the Bulls had defeated the Charlotte Hornets in four games in their first round series. Despite the Magic's superior record, many felt that the Bulls would win.

Also "battling" were Reebok (whom Shaq endorsed) and Nike (whom Jordan endorsed). With Shaq, Reebok had increased its share of the basketball shoe market from 15 to 18 percent, but Nike and Jordan were still the unquestioned leaders with 45 percent. Both companies played down the shoe rivalry as part of the basketball rivalry, but many observers still made the comparison. In addition, Michael Jordan, with his $30 million annually, and Shaquille O'Neal, with his $12.5 million, were Number 1 and 2 in the *Forbes* magazine listing of highest-paid athletes in the world.

Game one was in Orlando in the best of seven series, and Phil Jackson, coach of the Bulls, decided to use the "hack-a-Shaq" defense throughout much of the game. This strategy meant that the Chicago defender would foul Shaq and send him to the free-throw line, rather than let him take a shot for a sure two points. The Bulls had three centers, giving them 18 fouls to use against Shaq inside. Shaq threw off the strategy by sinking his first six free-throw attempts in the first quarter, then finishing with 12 of 16 for the game. He finished with 26 points and 12 rebounds and the Magic won, 94 to 91. Still, Chicago was heartened by the fact that it was only Shaq's good free-throw shooting that had prevented their victory. They planned to use the "hack-a-Shaq" strategy again in the next game, figuring his mediocre free-throw shooting for the year (53%) would be more likely in subsequent games.

Game two was all Michael Jordan as he scored 38 points in the 104 to 94 Chicago victory in Orlando. Shaq got 25 points and was 13 of 20 from the free-throw line, somewhat thwarting the Bulls' strategy. Shaq's teammates, however, shot the team out of the game, hitting just 10 of 25 from the field in the decisive last quarter, with Shaq getting only four shots. This loss led some observers to see the demise of the Magic in this series. Kareem Abdul-Jabbar, the Hall of Famer who was doing commentary on TNT for the series, said that he thought Orlando was in big trouble and that their lack of playoff experience was catching up to them. The Magic, however, were not intimidated. The Magic won Game three in Chicago by a score of 110 to 101, despite 40 points (but just 9 in the second half) from Jordan. Shaquille had 28 points, 10 rebounds, and hit two key free throws with 43 seconds left to secure the victory.

Shaquille may have been more inspired to show what he could do against the Bulls after the All-NBA teams were announced mid-way through the series. Shaquille was edged by David Robinson for the first team at center, with Hakeem Olajuwon chosen for the third team. Whether this result would be duplicated in the most valuable player voting wouldn't be known for another month. Meanwhile game four was to be played in Chicago and, in that contest, the Bulls evened the series at two games each by winning 106 to 95. The Bulls changed tactics and double or triple teamed Shaq each time he touched the ball, forcing him to give up the ball. This led to nine assists for Shaq, a career high, but it also limited his shooting (5 of 10 shots) and his points. His 17 points were 12 below his season average. Nevertheless, the Magic players were upbeat and ready to return to Orlando for a pivotal game.

Game five was a rugged contest, but the Magic and Shaquille came out on top, 103 to 95. Shaq had 23 points, 22 rebounds, and 5 blocks, although he returned to his poor free-throw shooting, going 9 for 19 from the line. Shaq began the game going 2 for 12 from the field, but finished strong. Horace Grant, continuing a great series against his old team, had 24 points, 11 rebounds, and played his usual strong defense. With the victory, the teams returned to Chicago where the Magic ended Jordan's efforts at a complete comeback to another NBA title by defeating them, 108 to 102. Most observers said that the Magic was the younger team who was fresher in the series, and the Bulls seemed to be aging. Shaq had 27 points and 13 rebounds and brought the Magic back from a 95 to 92 deficit with just over six minutes remaining. The victory led some to predict a Magic championship, although Orlando still had to beat either New York or Indiana to even get to the NBA finals.

The Indiana Pacers-New York Knicks series went to seven games before the Pacers triumphed. The Magic-Pacers series started two days later, with the Magic well rested after five days off. On the day that the series began, the most valuable player award was announced, and it went to David Robinson of the San Antonio Spurs, with Shaquille a distant second. This choice was largely based on the fact that the Spurs, with 62 wins, had the best record in the league, because Shaq had led the league in scoring, with Robinson third, and Shaq was third in rebounds to Robinson's seventh. Robinson had led Shaq in blocks, finishing fourth and sixth, respectively, but Shaq was second in field goal percentage and Robinson was not among the league leaders. Shaq directed his disappointment in finishing second toward the Pacers. In Game one he had 32 points and 11 rebounds, outplaying 7'4" Rik Smits (17 points) as the Magic won, 105 to 101. After the game, Shaq was pleased about the triumph and was able to laugh about his not winning the MVP award saying, "Boo-hoo, boo-hoo, oh, I didn't win the MVP. What am I going to do? Boo-hoo."[1]

In the second game the Shaq onslaught continued as he had 39 points, 17 in the fourth quarter, to propel the Magic to a 119–114 victory. In the two Magic victories Shaq hit 19 of 27 free throws (70%). The two teams traveled to Indianapolis for games three and four. There the Pacers put their game back together and won both games as Shaq was held to 18 points, 6 rebounds, and just 4 free-throw attempts in game three and just 16 points in game four. Even worse, he missed all eight of his free throws, as the Magic lost 94 to 93. He was limited to about 30 minutes of playing time in each game because of foul trouble, which brought criticism from many in the Magic camp. The series was down to the best of three as the teams returned to Orlando.

Pepsi chose to debut a new commercial featuring Shaq and (through special effects) classic film stars such as Cary Grant and Lucille Ball. Shaq then performed his own "special effects" as he scored 35 points and had 19 rebounds. He still had five fouls (one short of fouling out), but, after talking with Coach Brian Hill, Shaq let the game come to him; that is, he didn't try to force plays that weren't easily there. In game six the home team won again (as they had done throughout the series) with Indiana embarrassing the Magic, 123–96. Shaq scored 26 points, but the Pacers' shooting was red-hot as they cruised to a lead of 91 to 56 in the third quarter. The Eastern title would be decided in a seventh game in Orlando.

In Orlando the Magic reversed the hot shooting of Indiana and pummeled the Pacers by a score of 105 to 81. Besides leading the team with 25 points and 11 rebounds, Shaq also led them in a team dance after the victory. The starters shot 67 percent from the floor, and the game was never close in the second half after a seven-point Magic lead at halftime.

Shaq and the Magic had won the East and were four victories from an NBA championship. They would play the surprising Houston Rockets. The defending champions, after finishing as the sixth seed in the West, had proceeded to knock off Utah, with the second best record in the league in Round One, and Phoenix, the Pacific champion in Round Two after being down three games to one. They then met the Number 1 seeded Spurs and won their series, four games to two. The Rockets were a hot team, but Shaquille and the Magic felt confident that they could defeat them.

THE NBA FINALS, 1995

The NBA and the television networks that carry the NBA finals hope that the teams that make the finals will draw large numbers of viewers because the higher the ratings, the better for the network and the greater likelihood that the NBA will be able to negotiate a higher price for future playoffs. The best way to ensure high ratings is by having teams from large markets (New York, Chicago, Los Angeles) in the finals. This, of course, happens only occasionally, but another way to attract large viewer audiences is by having well-known stars in the playoffs, especially those who are very popular. Michael Jordan was one such player as were Charles Barkley, Larry Bird, and Magic Johnson. This finals match-up seemed likely to draw lots of viewers, despite the relatively small market audience of Houston and the much smaller audience of Orlando because it featured a battle between Shaquille O'Neal (the most popular of players) and Hakeem Olajuwon (less known among casual fans, but dominating when at the top of his game, which he was). A number of writers were favoring Orlando after they had upended Michael Jordan and the Bulls, as well as the Indiana Pacers. More writers, however, were influenced by Houston's march through the top teams in the West. One position-by-position breakdown had Houston favored at every position: Hakeem over Shaq, Robert Horry over Horace Grant, Mario Elie over Dennis Scott at small forward, Kenny Smith over Penny Hardaway at the point, Clyde Drexler over Nick Anderson at shooting guard, the Rocket bench and coaching staff over the Magic's. These predictions were based on past performances.

Game one was a great overtime thriller, which the Magic were poised to win. In the second quarter the Magic opened up a 20-point lead, but the Rockets refused to fold. They got five three-point shots from Kenny Smith in the third quarter and hit 14 of 32 as a team as they came back to take a 96 to 87 lead. Then the Magic came back and had a 110 to 107 lead with 10 seconds left in the game. Nick Anderson, who scored 22 points and had 11 rebounds, went to the line for two free throws and missed them both. Then, after Orlando rebounded the ball, Anderson was fouled again and missed two more free throws. Another three-pointer by Kenny Smith with 1.6 seconds left sent the game into overtime. Hakeem Olajuwon, who had 31 points and 23 rebounds, tipped in a shot in the last second to give Houston a 120 to 118 victory. The ending was demoralizing for the young Magic squad. Shaq had scored 26 points, grabbed 16 rebounds, and had 9 assists and hit 6 of 9 free throws. Still, his comment at the end of the game was that the Magic were a strong team that would come back, but that he had to continue to play better and stronger and to try to dominate.

Game two was the night that Reebok chose to debut a new ad starring Shaq with highlights from his playoff performances. With an anticipated near record viewing audience for the game, the cost of the ad was more than $300,000 for the 30-second spot, almost as expensive as Super Bowl ads. Having Shaquille in the finals caused both Pepsi and Reebok to buy even more airtime for their ads. Game two, however, also went to Houston by a score of 117 to 106, despite 33 points from Shaquille and 32 from Penny Hardaway. The loss put the Magic down two games to none as they headed to Houston.

The team was clearly down, but it was announced on the day of game three, that despite the intensity of the playoffs, Shaquille had still found time to send more than a dozen pairs of shoes (dress shoes, basketball shoes, casual shoes) to a 14-year-old in Mississippi who had grown so fast that his mother couldn't afford to get him new size 20 pairs of shoes. Shaq had responded, continuing to serve another group of people whom he didn't even know.

Shaq's thoughtfulness made no difference to the Rockets as they consistently beat the Magic and Shaquille down the court in transition as the Rockets won 106 to 103. After the loss in game three, some writers noted the Magic's overall shortcomings in the series, but a number blamed Shaquille the most for the loss. He was criticized as being too slow on defense or not playing hard enough to win, which would seem to be unfair, considering that Shaq had averaged 29 points and 12 rebounds in the three games. Nevertheless, there were the same old stories that he couldn't lead a team to a championship, and it hurt him, although he did not respond in anger. Down three games to none, no one gave the Magic a chance in the series, and many thought that it would now be a four game sweep. And it was. Houston won the final game 113 to 101, and Olajuwon was voted the MVP in the NBA finals after scoring 35 points and 15 rebounds in the last game. Shaq had 25 points and graciously congratulated the Rockets, but noted that he'd "be back in this position (the finals)" many times."

In recalling this series, Shaq said that after the team won the Eastern Finals, they partied, practiced lackadaisically, and joked around, thinking that they'd defeat the older and much lower-seeded Rockets. Mentally, the collapse in game one severely affected the team's confidence, and the Magic altered their play in a manner that hurt them. After the loss, Shaq remembered what Coach Hill said about not forgetting the feeling of disappointment for when they returned to the finals again. But it wasn't to be and, within a year, Shaq was no longer with the Magic.

SHAQ'S MANY VENTURES: THE BUSY SUMMER OF 1995

Shaquille had big plans for the summer. First was a return to Baton Rouge to work on his degree, fulfilling a promise that he had made to his mother, Lucille. He also would practice daily in the LSU gym in an effort to extend his shooting range and not allow defenses to totally collapse on him inside. He would also work on his free-throw shooting with a free-throw expert.

Before embarking on this plan, however, Shaquille made a commercial for Taco Bell with Hakeem Olajuwon in which Shaq says that Hakeem is only good when he has his team behind him. Shaq challenges Hakeem to a one-on-one duel for $1 million. The ad was very popular and Taco Bell was flooded with requests to actually sponsor such a contest. Normally this would not have been possible under the NBA's collective bargaining agreement, but the agreement had expired over the summer and, rather than renegotiate quickly, the league locked the players out of team events and training camps.

Both players were represented by Leonard Armato, and there was this unusual "window of opportunity" so a one-on-one contest between Shaq and Hakeem was scheduled for September 30, available on Pay-Per-View, with the winner taking a million-dollar prize.

Before that event, however, there were other things that kept Shaq in the spotlight. The new Olympic dream team (for the 1996 Olympics in Atlanta) was officially named, and Shaquille and teammate Penny Hardaway were chosen for the team. Shaq would also find time to squeeze in some movie making after his classes ended. In this film, Shaq played a genie (Kazaam), accidentally freed from captivity by a boy being chased by neighborhood toughs. Shaq (Kazaam) saves the boy, but the movie was universally panned by reviewers. Of almost as much interest as making the movie was where Shaq would live while doing so. He already had settled into a lakeside mansion in Orlando that was 22,000 square feet of living space in a gated community. It included 17 bedrooms, an indoor pool, a basketball court, an eight-seat movie theatre, and a recording studio. The home that Shaq was leasing in Beverly Hills for the four months of shooting (at $20, 000 per month) was much smaller (only 5,000 square feet) and had a tennis court and an area for shooting baskets, something Shaq especially wanted.

The filming went well and Shaq continued to work out, including time with a personal trainer with whom he did aerobics, martial arts, and boxing. These workouts made Shaq even stronger and that, combined with his shooting practice, made him ready for the one-on-one with Hakeem at the end of September. The "event" got quite a bit of media coverage, with most sportswriters saying that it seemed crazy for anyone to pay $20 to $25 to watch this competition. As it developed, the match grew into a series of matches pitting guards against guards and rookies against rookies. The NBA announced that this kind of event would not be allowed under any subsequent labor agreement. On the eve of the big match, Hakeem Olajuwon announced that he was pulling out after injuring his back while lifting weights. So the contest never took place and attention now turned for pro basketball fans to the beginning of a new NBA season.

NOTE

1. John P. Lopez, "MVP Aside, Shaq Stacks Up This Year? Maturing O'Neal, Magic Seek 2-0 Edge on Pacers Tonight," *Houston Chronicle*, May 25, 1995, 1.

Chapter 8

ONE MORE SHOT AT A TITLE

The 1995–1996 season opening was marked by some unusual events. After the league lockout and the new contract, the NBA referees went on strike during preseason until a new contract was negotiated. The replacement referees were challenged on nearly every call and lost control of a number of games. The Magic were picked to repeat as Atlantic Division champions, but the Chicago Bulls were selected as the likely Central Division and Eastern Conference champions. This was based on the return for an entire season of Michael Jordan, as well as the acquisition by the Bulls of Dennis Rodman, who had won four consecutive rebounding titles but had worn out his welcome in San Antonio because of his eccentric behavior.

The Magic had their whole team back but had not added anyone of any significance other than Jon Koncak, a veteran center who was acquired to provide backup for Shaquille at center. The acquisition took on significance when Matt Geiger of the Miami Heat committed a flagrant foul on Shaquille in an exhibition game. The result was a broken thumb for Shaquille and a suspension for a game and a $10,000 fine against Geiger. Shaquille would be sidelined for two months until around Christmas, following thumb surgery, and there was great fear that the Magic would not be able to win consistently without Shaq. Coach Hill sounded optimistic, saying that he didn't think that the team's play would let down in Shaquille's absence.

Brian Hill was right. After the first month of the season, Orlando had 13 wins and 2 losses, the top record in the East, even better than Chicago's 12 wins and 2 losses in the Central Division. The Magic players were playing like a team and preparing to improve even more when Shaquille returned. On December 14, the Magic played in Chicago against the Bulls and the Chicagoans triumphed 112 to 103. The win gave the Bulls a record of 17 and 2, while the loss dropped the Magic to 17 and 5, the second best record in the league. Despite the loss, things were looking up as Shaquille was scheduled to return the next game.

Orlando went six and one after Shaquille's return to finish 1995 with a record of 23 wins and 6 losses, 3 1/2 games ahead of the Knicks in the Atlantic Division. The Bulls led the Central Division with a 25 and 3 record. Shaquille averaged around 25 points and 11 rebounds per game as he played his way back into the shape he and the Magic wanted. He may have rushed this recovery a bit, because in early January, Shaquille suffered a strained left quadriceps muscle, which sidelined him for four games.

Shaq returned once again on January 15 and scored 33 points in Dallas, but the Mavericks had better balanced scoring in their 119–104 victory over Orlando. The Magic had a road record of 8 wins and 10 losses, but were undefeated at home at 20 and 0. Much of the Magic's success was due to the fine year that Shaq's best buddy, Dennis Scott, was having. Finally having the year many had expected of him, Scott was averaging just over 20 points, 4 rebounds, and 3 assists per game. With Shaq in and out of the lineup other players excelled, with Dennis Scott and Penny Hardaway having the most impact.

The NBA All-Star game lineups, as voted by the fans, were announced at the end of January, and both Penny and Shaq were named starters for the East squad, even though Shaq had missed almost half of his team's games. Shaq's presence in commercials, his clear dominance in games and his personality kept him at the forefront of the fans' thinking, and he easily outpolled Alonzo Mourning and Patrick Ewing for the starting center position. The Magic had the second best record in the East at 34 and 14 at the all-star break, with the Chicago Bulls, the best in the East and the league at 44 wins and only five losses. Phil Jackson, the Chicago coach, thus earned the right to coach the Eastern squad.

The same day that the full all-star rosters were announced, it was learned that Shaquille had been fined $5,000 by the league for "failing to leave the court in a timely manner and for verbally abusing the referees after he was ejected from the Magic's 102–79 loss at Indiana." This was also the day after Shaq had one of his best overall games, as he had scored 30 points, grabbed 19 rebounds, and had 7 assists in the 104 to 99 victory over the Celtics. One big negative was the return of Shaq's free-throw mishaps, as he went 2 of 13 from the line. The win improved the Magic home record for the year to 22 and 0 (29 straight over two seasons).

It was turning into an inconsistent season for Shaq and his teammates. Shaq was in and out of the lineup but was often great. His free-throw shooting was still a big problem (47% for the year). He was frustrated more by his injuries and the rough play and was retaliating more, resulting in more foul calls and ejections. Still, he was averaging about 26 points and 11 rebounds per game. The Magic were undefeated at home, but less than a .500 team on the road (9–14), which would not bode well in the payoffs were they to play the Chicago Bulls, who were winning almost every time they played.

The 1996 NBA All-Star game was played in San Antonio on February 11. The game was a close contest until the East, led by Shaq and Michael, pulled away for a 129 to 118 victory. Shaq was having a great time in this his fourth and best all-star game, played before lots of the hometown San Antonio crowd. He finished with 25 points (to lead all scorers) and 10 rebounds, culminating with a ferocious dunk over David Robinson that was acknowledged as the play of the game. Jordan had 20 points in only 22 minutes of action and was voted the most valuable player, by a vote of 4 to 3, by the seven media representatives who made the decision. The announcement sent a cascade of boos throughout the arena. Even Jordan acknowledged that Shaq probably deserved to win the award, but Michael had no say in the matter. Shaq tried to act unfazed saying, "I don't get upset. I get even. I don't get no respect." Later he said that he might not play in any more all-star games, but instead, spend the time with his family.

Two nights later, after destroying the Denver Nuggets with 30 points and 12 rebounds in a 28-point Magic victory, Shaq said that he wasn't mad any more, although he refused to talk to the media after the game. The Magic victory put them within one of the NBA record for consecutive home wins at the start of a season set in 1946–1947 (when the league was still the Basketball Association of America or BAA) by the Washington Capitols. That record fell on February 20 against Utah, as Shaq, with 24 points and 13 rebounds, led the Magic to a 123 to 104 rout of the Jazz.

Shaq also was the star of another new Taco Bell commercial, released that week, for an ultra-hot Taco, which he said he uses to "fire up" before playing. In the ad, he's then shown in flames as he slam dunks the basketball. He then quips, "Is it hot in here or just me?" As both a player and a marketing tool, Shaq was hot. The Taco Bell contract was worth about $5 million to Shaq.

The Magic home winning streak stretched to 33 (for the season, 40, overall), and their overall record was 52 and 17, but they were still behind the Bulls, who had a record of 60 and 7. Despite Orlando's great record, there were rumors that Coach Brian Hill might be replaced if Orlando failed to get to the NBA finals once again. There was some feeling that he had lost control of his young team and, more important, Shaquille was said to have soured on Hill because of his catering to Penny Hardaway's wishes in how the team was running its offense and defense. With Shaquille slated to become a free agent at the end of the year, the Magic wanted to do whatever they could to retain him. In the February issue of *Esquire Magazine*, Michael Wilbon had done a feature on Shaquille, and he had suggested that Shaq might sign with the Lakers at the end of the year. In response to that, Shaq had declared that he loved Orlando and believed that he'd be there for most, if not the rest, of his NBA career. Still, the Magic were obviously concerned by these rumors of Shaquille leaving.

On March 26, the Magic's home winning streak ended in a loss to the Lakers, 113 to 91. The loss was disappointing, but the lead that the Magic had in the Atlantic Division was so great that they clinched the division title a few days later with a victory over the second-place New York Knicks. In that game, a 98 to 79 win, Shaquille had 32 points, including 10 of 13 from the foul line.

A FAMILY CRISIS CHANGES SHAQ'S SEASON

Things should have been great for Shaquille and the Magic, but suddenly they were not. In March, Shaq's grandmother (Lucille's mother), Odessa Chambliss, was hospitalized. She had been instrumental in raising Shaq, and he was worried and upset about her hospitalization. Shaq visited her in March and could see how thin and weak she was, but no one told him specifically that she was dying of cancer. He returned on April 2 when the Magic were scheduled to play the Knicks. When he went to her house she was in a coma, and the attending nurse told him that she would soon die.

Shaq cried by himself for about three hours, but then tried to put on a strong appearance so he could help his mother through this terrible time. His grandmother passed away that night and Shaq, for the first time in his 24 years, had lost someone close to him. He considered taking a month off because he was so distraught, but decided to rejoin the team after the funeral.

Shaquille returned to his grandmother's house on Sunday. He knew that she would have wanted him to play, but he was simply too disheartened to do so. Then his mother paged him and told him to play. With that, he boarded a plane and got into Orlando at around 5 pm, went immediately to the arena, and entered the court with about four minutes left in the first quarter. The Bulls led 28–21 after the first quarter when Shaquille entered the game. He finished with 21 points and 9 rebounds in his three quarters, but it wasn't enough, as the Bulls won, 90 to 86. The Magic had now lost three of their last four games at home.

Worse than the loss was the way Shaquille felt he was treated by the team. He felt that they weren't understanding enough about his loss and that some in the organization questioned his team loyalty for not coming back sooner. Coach Brian Hill stated that if Shaq wasn't there by tip-off, he wouldn't play on Sunday. Interviewed at halftime of the game, Brian Hill said that his remarks had been misconstrued, but Shaq was hurt. Whether the mention of disloyalty was true or not was less important than the fact that Shaquille felt slighted by the team, and this would be a significant factor at the end of the year when he became a free agent.

With the various division races pretty much decided, the next important events would involve the playoffs, which began at the end of April. Despite missing 28 games, Shaquille had still helped the magic to a record of 60 wins and 22 losses, three games better than the previous year and 13 ahead of New York in the Division. Shaquille had averaged 26.6 points per game, third in the league behind Michael Jordan and Hakeem Olajuwon. Shaq was also third in field goal percentage and ninth in blocks, but not among the top 10 in rebounds. His average of 11.0 would have been sixth, but he didn't play in enough games to qualify for listing in this category. His free-throw percentage had been under .500 (.487), something that continued to plague him.

The Magic, as the Number 2 seed, would play the Number 7 seed, the Detroit Pistons, in a best-of-five series. Detroit had played well against the Magic during the year, but Shaquille had missed a couple of the early season games, and the Pistons had ended their season not playing well. That latter pattern continued into the playoffs as Shaquille and the Magic swept the Pistons in three straight games. The first game was a 20-point victory, with Shaq scoring 21 points. Game two was won by a 92 to 77 score, and Shaq again led with 29 points. Game three was in Detroit and was closer, but the Magic won by a score of 101 to 98.

The swift series meant that the Magic would have eight days off before meeting the winner of the Atlanta-Indiana series. The team would appreciate the rest, but there was also the risk of getting "rusty" by going so long without playing. The team would practice but the intensity, both physical and mental, might not be there. With all that time off, it might seem that Shaq might get bored, but there seemed to be no risk of that. Shaq and his friends played what they called "apartment war games" in the early hours of the morning, using smoke bombs and paint ball. This was a manifestation of the eternal child in Shaq. At his $4 million home in Isleworth, Florida, Shaq often played video games with his visiting teenage siblings in his huge hi-tech room. In that room were pinball machines, video games, an air hockey machine, and a Pepsi vending machine that dispensed juice and soda at no charge. Celebrities and teammates often dropped by to play with Shaq's various "toys." Included in that definition would be Shaq's home recording studio where he was preparing tracks for his third CD.

The week off seemed to have no effect on the Magic when they opened the series in Orlando against the Atlanta Hawks, the upset victor over Indiana in five games. Orlando opened with a 117–105 victory over the Hawks. Shaq had 41 points and 13 rebounds in the victory. Two nights later, the Magic made it two in a row with a 120 to 94 win. Shaq was double-teamed even more, but still had 28 points to lead Orlando.

The Magic had now won five playoff games in a row, and they also seemed to have overcome their early road woes, having won eight of their last nine regular season games away from Orlando. Still, some critics felt Shaq was not giving enough attention to basketball. He was defended, again, by his General Manager, John Gabriel, as well as by several of his teammates, who lauded his keen mind and competitive nature. There was no denying, however, that Shaq's free-throw shooting needed significant improvement, something freely and painfully acknowledged by Shaquille, himself.

Game three in Atlanta was another Magic victory in which Shaq had team highs of 24 points and 17 rebounds and left Orlando one game from winning another series. Eying a sweep, the Magic stumbled a bit in game four, losing 104 to 99. Shaq took the bulk of the blame for that loss, despite scoring 19 points and taking down 8 rebounds. His failure was at the free-throw line, once again, where he made only 5 of 17 attempts. He vowed to dunk the ball every time he got it the next game, guaranteeing that the Magic would win the game. During the game Shaq also experienced an unusual sensation, which seemed to be an irregular heartbeat. Examined by doctors at halftime, he seemed to be fine and later examinations by heart specialists indicated that he was probably suffering from stress.

Totally cleared to play, Shaq dunked, swooped, and dominated, finishing with 27 points and snaring 16 rebounds in the 96 to 88 victory. With the win, the Magic headed to Chicago to play the Bulls, who had eliminated the Knicks in five games. The Bulls had set an NBA record for victories with 72 and had defeated Orlando in three of four contests during the season. Shaq had missed two of these games and arrived late for a third, so it was difficult to determine what the season record really meant. Observers were split on their views of the outcome, with most favoring Chicago.

The series was never very close as the Bulls swept the Magic in four games, then went on to win another NBA title. Game one was a rout, with Chicago winning by 121 to 83, even though Shaq had 27 points and Penny Hardaway had 38 points. Even worse, Horace Grant collided with Shaq and suffered a hyperextended elbow, which knocked Grant out of the rest of the series. Game two was closer and the Magic even had an 18-point lead early in the second half before the Bulls went on a 21 to 5 run and won by 93 to 88. Shaquille had 26 points at the half, but his team-mates failed to get him the ball much in the third quarter when he took only three shots, finishing the game with 36 points and 16 rebounds.

The two teams traveled to Orlando where game three was even worse for the Magic. The Bulls held Hardaway to 18 and Shaq to 17 points, and Shaq helped them by shooting one of nine from the free-throw line. The score was 86 to 67. Game four was an improvement, but the Bulls won, 106 to 101, to end the series. Shaq finished with 28 points, but exploded in angry frustration in the locker room after the game. He refused to shake hands with the Chicago players, stormed off the court, and hurled a chair in the locker room. As soon as the game ended the question on many people's minds was "would Shaq return to Orlando?" He said that Orlando was his first option, but he would take at least a week to make a decision. He officially would be a free agent on July 1. This would be one of the big stories in basketball during the summer. The other big story would be the Olympic Games in Atlanta, beginning July 20.

SHAQ SIGNS WITH THE LAKERS

The pursuit of Shaq by Orlando was, to Shaq, a bit insulting at times. He announced, half in jest and half seriously, that he expected $150 million for the length of his contract. A number of fans were quite put off by this declaration, and some paid for billboards in the city that said, "Is Shaq worth $150 million?" In the negotiations, the Magic noted that they couldn't give Shaq more than Penny because it would upset Penny. Shaq and Penny had gotten along well for three years, and Shaq had supported Penny when he had held out for a larger contract. Shaq didn't get the same support from Penny, and he was angry that the team felt that Penny was more valuable than he. An Orlando radio station made insulting comments about Shaq and the relationship with his girlfriend, who was about to have his second child, Taahirah. Finally all the insults, the financial disappointment, and the fact that other players on the market (particularly Alonzo Mourning) were getting far more than Orlando was offering led to Shaq's decision to sign with the Lakers. After the Lakers cut a number of players and freed up a great deal of money, Shaq signed for $121 million over seven years. The contract was signed in Atlanta at the Olympic Games.

Shaq left with a lot of bitterness both on his part and that of the local fans, but he also had tired of being the proverbial big fish in a small pond. He was looking forward to blending in more in Los Angeles, at least as much as a guy 7'1" and 330 pounds can blend in anywhere.

The 1996 U.S. Olympic team was termed Dream Team II to distinguish itself from the original dream team of 1992, when NBA players were first eligible for the U.S. Olympic basketball team. That team, with Michael Jordan, Magic Johnson, Larry Bird, and Charles Barkley, had blown through the Olympic field and set the world on notice that the American Olympic team was back to its old dominance. This 1996 team, when announced in February, had drawn similar responses. Vlade Divac, the Lakers' center and an Olympian for his native Yugoslavia said, "Second is not so bad," meaning that he was already conceding the gold medal to the United States. Divac would be traded in June to Charlotte for the Number 13 draft pick, a high schooler named Kobe Bryant, who would turn out to be a key to Shaq and the Lakers' later success.

This new U.S. Olympic team included John Stockton, David Robinson, Hakeem Olajuwon (a naturalized U.S. citizen), Reggie Miller, Charles Barkley, and Karl Malone. Shaq, however, was the biggest star of the team, literally and figuratively. Not only Shaq's size but his placement on an enormous mural on the side of an historic building in Atlanta made him the "picture" of the Atlanta Olympics. Buena Vista Pictures had also decide to release "Kazaam," the film that Shaq had made the previous summer, during the Olympics to capitalize on his Olympic presence.

Because of the Olympics, Shaq would not enroll at LSU during the summer term. His movement toward his college degree, promised to his parents, would be on hold for another summer. The speculation about where he'd land for his next NBA season dominated the NBA news in June. When it came down to Orlando or Los Angeles, there was speculation supporting each team. Besides all the other factors, Shaq wanted to go with the team that had the greatest chance of winning a championship with him. William C. Rhoden noted that the Laker legacy of great centers from George Mikan to Wilt Chamberlain to Kareem Abdul-Jabbar, all of whom won NBA championships with the Lakers, might be the edge that the Lakers needed to sign Shaq.[1] The Olympic squad assembled about two weeks before the Games began in Atlanta. Shaq managed to squeeze in a surprise performance with rapper Notorious B.I.G. in Chicago, where the team was practicing. Then the squad played five exhibition games, one of which was very close, against a team of collegiate all-stars. Before getting themselves righted, the Olympians trailed 59 to 42 at the half, but eventually won the game 96 to 90. The other four exhibitions, played against other national teams, were not as close. They won the last game, against Greece, in Atlanta 128 to 62. Covered as much as the game was the continued speculation of where Shaquille, John Stockton, and other unsigned NBA stars would play the next year. Signing Shaquille in Atlanta put a lot of the stories behind and allowed the Olympics to receive coverage without any "interference" from the NBA signing stories, which were everywhere in the days immediately preceding the opening of the Olympic Games.

As expected the American team ran roughshod through the Olympics, but it wasn't always pretty and, sometimes, it was even boring. The fans at the games were not very loud, except when there was a thunderous dunk, a number of which were provided by Shaquille. Generally, however, the U.S. team didn't arouse the kind of awe and admiration the original dream team had, despite winning all of their Olympic contests. A defeat of Lithuania was 104 to 82, but the game was tied at 40 before the U.S. team seemed to finally apply themselves. A rout of China was 133 to 70. Their sixth win was against Brazil, 98 to 75, and it sent them into the semifinals against Australia. Again the Americans won easily, 101–73. With all the great U.S. stars, Shaquille didn't really distinguish himself, except by his trademark dunks. Charles Barkley had 24 points in the game, but in most U.S. wins, it was unusual to have anyone get that many points, because all of the squad was playing about equal minutes. Robinson, Penny Hardaway, and Shaq all had 14 in the contest. The championship match was similar, as the U.S. team defeated Yugoslavia, 95 to 69. Shaq and Penny sparked the listless U.S. team, down 34 to 33, to a 46 to 36 lead at the half. The U.S. team was never threatened again and pulled away throughout the half to the final 26-point victory. Shaq said he learned a lot from playing in the Olympics, but mostly from practicing with and against his U.S. teammates.

Immediately after the Olympics, Shaq returned to California, both because it was his new home and because he was starring in another film, "Steel," based on a minor DC Comics hero. This film would be released in the summer of 1997 to mediocre reviews for both the film and Shaq's acting. Nevertheless, he enjoyed the filming and prepared to return to basketball when training camp opened in October. This was a new opportunity for Shaquille and he hoped that an NBA title would finally come from it.

NOTE

1. William C. Rhoden, "A Course in History, Not Econ," *New York Times*, April 30, 1996, B11.

Chapter 9

SHAQ IS A LAKER

In 1996, the Lakers had finished with a record of 53 and 29, good for second in the Pacific Division, but they were eliminated by Houston in the first round of the playoffs. The acquisition of Shaquille was supposed to dramatically improve the team, but, in order to sign him, a number of players from the team were traded or cut, leaving the Lakers with little depth and untested players such as 18-year-old Kobe Bryant, the youngest player in NBA history. As early as July, there were those who noted that the Lakers would need a lot more to win an NBA title. In August at his first Laker workout, Shaq stated that he wanted to come into the season as a "lean, mean dunking machine," what he called the "old Shaq." One early "casualty" for the Lakers was the loss of Coke as a corporate sponsor of the team and the Great Western Forum where the Lakers played. Because of Shaq's exclusive agreement with Pepsi, Coke pulled out of its agreement with the Lakers. It was assumed that Pepsi would take their place as the exclusive cola sold at Lakers games.

The NBA television schedule was released in July, and Shaq's presence was acknowledged by the L.A. Lakers playing the Phoenix Suns on the opening night of the season as part of a double header on TNT. TNT also would broadcast the Magic's first visit to L.A. to face their old teammate on the Lakers on December 6, and NBC would air their rematch in Orlando, which would be Shaq's "homecoming," on March 23.

The Bulls had been picked to win the Central Division and the Eastern Conference. Orlando was expected to fall to second in the Atlantic Division behind New York. In the West, Houston was picked to edge Utah in the Midwest Division, and Seattle was the choice in the Pacific over the

Lakers. The rest of the division was seen as rebuilding. The Lakers were coached by Del Harris, a 59-year-old who had been the head coach of the Houston Rockets for four years and the Milwaukee Bucks slightly more than four years before taking the Lakers' position in 1994. He was generally a tactician who emphasized defense and was a very polite, low-key individual. That would change at times as the Lakers frustrated him with selfish play during his coaching tenure.

The exhibition games would be the first time that Shaq had competed with his new teammates in a real contest, and his debut was very positive. Shaq had 25 points on 11 of 13 shooting and 12 rebounds as the Lakers topped the Denver Nuggets in Honolulu. Both the Nuggets' coach and Del Harris praised Shaquille's play. The next game, also against Denver in Honolulu, was even more impressive, as Shaq had 27 points, 15 rebounds, and 9 assists, falling just one short of getting a "triple-double" in the Lakers' 105 to 96 win.

By the time the season started on November 1, Shaq had become the newest celebrity in a city with lots of them. He was the most visible, however; even in restaurants or clubs filled with celebrities, Shaq's entrance drew a crowd of greeters. His presence had excited the fans and led to an increase of more than 3,600 season ticket holders for the new season, despite a huge increase in ticket prices. With the birth of his new daughter, Shaq said that he'd be more of a homebody, although he said that he would refuse to answer questions about his personal life. He acknowledged that he would be driving more carefully now and had left his Porsche behind, settling on a light truck instead.

The Lakers opened their regular season in Los Angeles, against the Phoenix Suns, with a 96 to 82 victory, as Shaquille scored 23 points and retrieved 14 rebounds. The Lakers then went on the road to Madison Square Garden in New York where a sellout crowd of 19,763 turned out to witness what some said might be a preview of the NBA finals, with Shaq and the Lakers against Patrick Ewing and the Knicks. The game was close until the last minute when the Lakers pulled away to win, 98 to 92. Shaquille had 26 points and 13 rebounds.

The next day, the NBA announced its 50 top players of all time, a news release made to coincide with what the NBA was calling its 50th anniversary. The top 50 players would be introduced as part of the ceremonies of the NBA All-Star game to be played in February in Gund Arena in Cleveland. Shaquille, along with rivals Patrick Ewing, David Robinson, and Hakeem Olajuwon, were all named as members of this elite team. The Lakers and Shaq hoped that he'd be at the all-star game as a player and not just as a member of this team to be introduced at halftime.

The rest of the month was uneven for the Lakers, who still seemed to be learning how to play well together. By the end of the month, Shaq was averaging just under 25 points and just over 13 rebounds per game and hitting 44 percent of his free throws. The Lakers were at 11 wins and 6 losses, three games behind Seattle in the Pacific Division.

Shaq also continued to do the charitable work that had his own personal stamp on it. Just before Christmas, he donned a Santa hat and handed out donated toys at a community center in Watts, one of the poorest neighborhoods of Los Angeles. Being "Shaqa-Claus" kept up the tradition he had started with visiting sick children in hospitals, donating clothing to needy kids, and sponsoring meals for the homeless at "Shaqs-giving".

As 1997 began, Coach Del Harris was still trying to find the best combinations to ensure the success of the Lakers during the regular season and into the playoffs. Early in January he inserted 18-year-old Kobe Bryant for 22 minutes against the Sacramento Kings, and Bryant responded with 21 points. Harris said that he had expected that this would happen and looked for more performances like this from young Bryant.

Shaquille had sprained his right ankle and missed this game, then returned to play against Vancouver. Unfortunately he sprained the left ankle in that next game. This injury "jinx" was new and frustrating for Shaquille. In his first three years in the NBA, he had missed only two games. Then he was out 18 games in his last year in Orlando. He had hoped that the move to L.A. would mean his injuries were behind him, but that was not working out the way he had envisioned. Despite the injured ankles, he played 40 minutes against the Vancouver Grizzlies and scored 31 points. After the game he sat on the trainer's table with both ankles in a big bucket of ice.

The next night Shaq played 40 more minutes against the Portland Trailblazers after having two physical therapy sessions earlier in the day. His ankles were wrapped tightly, but he still scored 34 points and grabbed 12 rebounds in an 88 to 84 loss. This snapped the Lakers' win streak at six, leaving their record at 25 wins and 10 losses. The Lakers' success seemed directly related to their new additions—Shaquille and the three rookies, Kobe Bryant, Derek Fisher, and Travis Knight.

Shaquille's excellent year, which had him second in scoring, third in blocked shots, and fourth in both rebounding and field goal percentage, earned him a spot on the all-star team once again. For the first time, however, he would not be a starter, having finished second in the fan voting to Hakeem Olajuwon. Shaq said that he had no problem with that decision because Hakeem was a "class act."

INJURIES TO SHAQUILLE

By the end of January, the Lakers (33–12) had a one-game lead on Seattle (32–13) in the Pacific Division. Then in February the team and Shaq were devastated when Shaquille injured his knee and was out for two months, returning at the end of the regular season.

Shaq's knee problems began in Los Angeles in a game against the Washington Bullets. In the third quarter, Shaq bumped into Georges Muresan and suffered what was called a strained right knee. It turned out to be a sprained ligament. He had scored 24 points in 31 minutes of play when he was injured. Shaq missed the next game, which the Lakers managed to win easily against the Chicago Bulls, ending the Bulls' eight-game win streak. Shaq was forced to miss the all-star game, but he returned to action 10 days after his knee strain to play against the Timberwolves in Minnesota on February 12. Four minutes into the game his left knee buckled after he grabbed a rebound. Shaq recovered, apparently, and stayed in the game, scoring eight points in the next four minutes, but then left the game and was taken to the locker room. Shaq returned to Los Angeles where doctors determined that he had a partially torn ligament, a hyperextended joint, torn tissue around the left knee, and a fractured bone. He was fitted with a splint that he would wear for the next two to three weeks, but he would be able to avoid surgery.

Shaq's absence would surely affect the Lakers adversely. They were in first place in the Pacific Division with the best record in the Western Conference at 37 and 13. It seemed unlikely that they could continue to play so well without Shaquille. By the end of February, they had fallen to second in the division, after winning two of their previous seven games; they were now 39 and 18.

Shaquille returned to his Isleworth home, outside Orlando, for much of his recovery. As he did with most things, he worked hard on rehabilitating his knee. In early March the results of his hard work at rehabbing were apparent when he showed up at a Laker practice session on his 25th birthday (March 6th) and was able to do some short sprinting. He said that he would be able to play on April 2 against the Denver Nuggets. Of course, O'Neal would not be allowed to play with the Lakers until the doctors working with him okayed that return to action.

Shaquille's timeline for his return was a bit optimistic, but he still was back for a full practice on April 7. He was evaluated later in the week and cleared to return on April 11 for a game in Los Angeles against the Phoenix Suns. Playing only 24 minutes, he managed to score 24 points, snare 11 rebounds, and block 3 shots, as the Lakers topped the Suns, 114 to 98.

Shaq had been out 58 days and had missed 28 games, so he was tired after the game. He noted that he would get stronger as he played more, which would come after the doctors lifted restrictions on how long he could play in a game. Two nights later he played 41 minutes, after the restrictions were lifted, scored 39 points, grabbed 13 rebounds, and hit the game-winning shot at the buzzer as the Lakers won over the Utah Jazz, 100 to 98.

The Lakers and Shaquille made it three in a row with a 108 to 99 win over the Sacramento Kings four nights later. Shaquille played 33 minutes, had 42 points, 12 rebounds, and made 12 of 14 free throws. The resurgent Lakers were again looking to win the Pacific Division.

With the division title on the line, the Lakers slipped a bit by losing to the Trail Blazers, 100 to 96. The loss gave Seattle the division title and dropped the Lakers to the Number 4 seed for the Western Conference Playoffs. Shaquille had 24 points, but missed two free throws with 1.2 seconds left to seal the Lakers' fate. The loss would match the Lakers against the same Portland team in the first round of the playoffs, five days later.

THE 1997 PLAYOFFS

The first two games were played in Los Angeles, and the Lakers routed the Blazers in both games. In the first game, Shaquille was unstoppable, scoring 46 points, a career high, in just 35 minutes and also taking 11 rebounds. In game two, Shaq was double and triple teamed, but still got 30 points and 5 assists.

The teams went to Portland and the Blazers put together one good game, winning 98 to 90. Shaquille continued his hot scoring with 29 points to go along with 12 rebounds, and Kobe Bryant had his first big playoff game, with 22 points, but the Blazers would not allow a Laker sweep. One very disturbing incident was a flagrant foul committed on Shaquille by Blazers' center, Chris Dudley. Dudley defended the play, but many of the Lakers were upset over the action. Shaq declined to speak to reporters after practice the next day. Instead, he let his actions in game four speak for him, as he scored 27 points to lead the team. The Lakers, last in the league in free-throw shooting, made 38 of 44 free throws (86%) to seal the team victory. They would now face the Utah Jazz, who had swept the Clippers in three games.

The Jazz were led by their perennial all-stars, Karl Malone and John Stockton, perhaps the greatest "pick and roll" tandem to ever play in the NBA. Their 64 and 18 record was, by far, the best in the Western Conference and only five games behind the Bulls' record of 69 and 13. The Jazz were rested, having been off for five days; the Lakers went right from

Portland to Salt Lake City to play two nights later. The Lakers looked fatigued in a 93 to 77 loss. Shaquille, double-teamed most of the game, had just 17 points. Game two was a heart-breaking loss for the Lakers, 103 to 101, in a very rough game. Shaq had 25 points, but made only 10 of 25 shots, missing a shot with 10 seconds left.

The two teams flew to Los Angeles where the Lakers clamped down on defense and the Jazz cooperated by shooting poorly when open. The result was a 104–84 Lakers' victory, but Shaquille played only 18 minutes because of foul trouble and was ejected after getting two technical foul calls after scoring just 11 points. Game four found the Jazz shooting well again and the Lakers looking like a team in disarray. Shaq finished with 34 points and 11 rebounds, but got little help from his teammates, who seemed to lack energy. Returning to Salt Lake City for game five, the Lakers were much more energized as the game went into overtime before the Jazz ended the series and the Lakers' year with a 98 to 93 win. Shaquille had 23 points and 13 rebounds, but fouled out with 1:46 left in regulation. At the end of the game, rookie Kobe Bryant seemed to take charge for the Lakers, but put up three air balls from three-point range as O'Neal, Robert Horry, and Byron Scott were all out of the game because of injuries or disqualifications. What had started as a promising season had been disappointing when Shaq was injured. Then, the Lakers came back strongly, only to self-destruct in this last series. Changes were likely to be made over the off-season.

Shaquille's off-season was bound to include more commercials and films. During the playoff series with the Jazz he and his mom, Lucille, were featured in a CBS special called "All-Star Moms," airing as part of Mother's Day. The two were filmed cooking together. Later in May Shaq filmed a Pepsi ad that co-starred Deion Sanders, Mia Hamm, racer Jeff Gordon, and volleyball Olympian, Holly McPeak. Shaq was also awarded a Life Enrichment Award from the Charles Drew University of Medicine and Science for his numerous contributions and personal appearances on behalf of children. There was a certain irony in this because a university award seemed to contrast with Shaq's lack of a college degree. He seemed not to need one, but he persevered another summer term at LSU, moving closer to earning the degree that he had promised his parents.

During the summer Shaquille worked out religiously, hoping that being in top shape might prevent a recurrence of the injuries that had plagued him the prior season. He also found time to do his charity work. In June he returned to Newark where he dedicated a playground as part of the 12th Festival of People, held in Newark each summer. Shaq purchased a new home in the Beverly Hills area of Los Angeles in July. Although it didn't have a basketball court, it did have 8 bedrooms, 14 bathrooms, an elevator, a tennis court, and a great view of Los Angeles. Shaq and his girlfriend, Arnetta Yardbourgh, and their one-year-old daughter would now be united. Arnetta had been finishing graduate work in Houston and the baby was living with her. Shaq's third rap CD, "You Can't Stop the Reign," on his own rap label, T.W.IsM., as well as the movie, "Steel" were released in the summer. Also released was a film in which Shaq had a cameo role as himself. The movie, "Good Burger," was a well-received comedy, based on a Nickelodeon sketch first seen on the hit series, "All That." Shaq also co-produced and narrated a new Nickelodeon series called "Sports Theater with Shaquille O'Neal." The shows would air Saturdays, beginning in October.

In the fall, Shaq traveled to Rio de Janeiro, Brazil, to promote basketball and Reebok shoes. In a demonstration at a sports center near a Rio slum, Shaq brought the gym's backboard crashing to the ground after a dunk. Because of this incident, the game was canceled, and Shaq left without talking to the hundreds of children who had gathered, hoping to speak to him. Shaq returned to the United States and training camp in Palm Desert, California, preparing for the new season. During that time 10 of the members of the new Dream Team IV, set to play in the World Championships in Athens, Greece the next summer of 1998, were announced. Shaquille was one of the members and the only center at that point. Early in training camp, Shaquille suffered what was called a strained abdominal muscle. It was not considered serious at the time, but it would plague him for most of the season. Shaquille was being looked to as the leader of the Lakers, and he was openly disappointed that he had not played and won an NBA finals series in his first five years in the league. He was inspired, however, by his general manager on the Lakers, Jerry West, one of the greatest players ever, who told Shaq that he (West) had gone to the finals eight times before winning a championship. Shaq appreciated West's encouragement and admired his patience, but Shaq said that he didn't feel like waiting that long. He wanted a championship in 1998.

A NEW SEASON WITH NEW HOPES

In the first exhibition game, Shaq's high scoring (25 points) was exceeded by Kobe Bryant's (31 points), indicating a dynamic one-two punch for the Lakers in the new season. The only significant addition to the team was Rick Fox, a free agent who had played five years for the Boston Celtics. Fox scored 12 points for the team in the opening exhibition game. In the next exhibition game, Shaq scored 27 more points, although the Lakers lost. Many writers were already picking the Lakers to win the Western Conference and to meet the Bulls in the finals.

The season started on a sour note for Shaquille, who lost his temper because of an opposing player's comments, and Shaq slapped the player during a shoot around before an exhibition game. This resulted in a fine and suspension for the season opener for Shaq. Total cost, including a game's pay, was $156,794. Then Shaq was out again with the abdominal strain he had suffered earlier and missed 8 of the first 11 games, all of which the Lakers won, one of the best starts in NBA history. The Lakers lost at Miami, but were 13 and 2 at the end of November, despite Shaquille being out for five more games. He attended practices and home games but had treatment twice a day for the strain, which can be career-threatening. Shaq came back and played much of the season, but he was nagged by this injury until December of the next season. He later wrote that "[I] was scared that I would never be able to play basketball like I once did."[1]

During November Shaq had also opened an apparel and marketing business in Compton, a working class city of the Los Angeles region with high unemployment and high minority population. The facility would employ about 40 people, and Shaq noted that his company was in Compton to create jobs and keep kids out of trouble.

Shaq missed another month of play, but at the end of 1997, the Lakers, at 23 and 7, were just a game back of Seattle (24 and 6) in the Pacific Division. Even without playing nearly the entire season, Shaquille was still the vote leader for the center position for the West in the all-star game. Shaquille's biggest competition at the position, Hakeem Olajuwon, was also out, having had knee surgery in late November. He was not scheduled to return until sometime in February.

Shaquille returned to the court on January 3 against the Atlanta Hawks. He was limited to 20 minutes of play by his doctors, but managed to play 24 minutes and score 22 points in a Lakers' victory. Without him the Lakers had gone 15 and 7, good but not good enough to win a championship. Within a week Shaquille's playing time was up to 36 minutes, as he scored 25 points and 14 rebounds in a victory over the Grizzlies in Vancouver. He wasn't playing at 100 percent of his ability, but was working back into shape. By the end of the month of January, the Lakers were 32 and 11 (17 and 4 with Shaq in the lineup) and were two games behind Seattle in the division. Shaquille was averaging about 26 points per game and looking forward to the all-star game in Madison Square Garden on February 8, a homecoming of sorts for Shaquille. The Lakers had two starters (Shaq and Kobe) and two reserves (Nick Van Exel and Eddie Jones) on the all-star team, more than any other team, as the league headed into the all-star break.

THE ALL-STAR GAME AND THE REST
OF THE 1997–1998 SEASON

The run-up to the all-star game dredged up some of the old "conspiracy theories" about Shaq and prior games. Shaq had always resented that in the basically, "non-defense" all-star games, he had not only been guarded, but often double teamed and had not won an MVP award in any of the games. He wanted to play well in New York, despite his long layoff before the game. Shaq played 18 minutes and got 12 points and 4 rebounds in a 135 to 114 loss to the East, but seemed to enjoy playing and watching the game.

After the game, there were the usual mid-season predictions about the rest of the year, and many writers saw the Lakers as maturing and gaining strength as Shaquille got into full shape. The key to the Lakers' success would be a more aggressive attitude, one that emulated what Shaquille seemed to portray in most games. Some Lakers said that the team needed to mature, and the rest of the season would give them that opportunity. Their first opportunity against the Pacific-leading Supersonics did not go well. Playing at home the Lakers failed to win in overtime, despite 44 points and 12 rebounds from Shaquille. The Sonics now had a three-game lead on the Lakers.

By the end of the month, the lead held steady as the Lakers won only 7 of 12 games in February. The Lakers finally got hot over the last six weeks of the season and won 22 of their last 27 games, with a record of 61 and 21, to tie the Supersonics for the Pacific Division title. Shaquille had some big scoring games in the last month to finish the year with a 28.3 point per game average and 11.4 rebounds per game. Because the Sonics' record against the Lakers was better than Lakers' against the Sonics, the Sonics received a higher seeding, pitting them against the Timberwolves and the Lakers against the Portland Trailblazers.

The Lakers and Shaquille, especially, wanted to get back to the NBA finals, and Shaquille was eager to win his first title. The series against Portland was a good start. The Blazers had given the Lakers lots of difficulty during the season, but the Lakers won the series in four games. The first two games, in Los Angeles, were close, but the Lakers swept them. In game one, the Lakers struggled, finally taking the lead at the end of the third period before winning, 104 to 102. Shaquille had 30 points to lead the scoring. In game two, Shaq had his lowest point total in six weeks (19), but his teammates finally rallied and the Lakers won easily by a score of 108–99.

During the day off for travel, the Lakers' owner, Dr. Jerry Buss, assured questioners that Coach Del Harris would return the next season. Shaquille liked Harris but was beginning to lose respect for his coaching. All would be forgotten, however, if the Lakers won the NBA title. Game three went to Portland, however, by a score of 99 to 95. As a team, the Lakers were only 19 of 35 from the free-throw line, and Shaquille was 4 of 12, despite scoring 36 points and getting 16 rebounds for the game. The series ended two nights later when the Lakers won for the first time in Portland that season by a 110 to 99 margin. Shaquille was fabulous, once again, with 31 points and 15 rebounds. With the victory, the Lakers would now face Seattle in four days, opening in Washington on May 4.

The Lakers and Shaquille looked unstoppable after losing the opening game of the series, 106 to 92. The Lakers then swept the next four games, with only one as close as 12 points. In three of the five games, Shaquille had at least 30 points, and he averaged 30.4 points and 9.6 rebounds in the series. In addition Harris and O'Neal mutually praised the other's contributions to the team's successes, indicating that Harris was likely to return as coach.

In the Western Conference finals, the Lakers would face the Utah Jazz, the same team that had beaten them in four of five games in the playoffs the year before. The Jazz had the best record in the West, so the series would begin in Salt Lake City after the Jazz beat the Spurs in five games. Most writers were picking the Lakers but with a caution, once expressed by Lakers' guard, Nick Van Exel, "if we play to our potential, we'll win." Unfortunately for Shaq and his teammates, they didn't do so, losing the series to the Jazz in four straight games, two of which weren't close.

Game one was a rout by a 112 to 77 score. Shaq had 19, but shot 6 of 16 with seven turnovers. The rest of the team was even worse. Game two was close before the Jazz prevailed, 99 to 95. Shaquille had 31 points but again had little help from the rest of the Lakers.

Returning to Los Angeles, the Lakers found out that the NBA had announced its postseason honors. Michael Jordan was voted the MVP for the fifth time, with Shaq finishing fourth in the balloting, despite missing 22 games. Shaquille was voted to the First Team as the center on the All-NBA teams. Eddie Jones was the only other Laker to get more than one vote in the balloting, illustrating how vital Shaq was to everything that the Lakers did. The score in game three was 109 to 98, with Shaquille scoring 39 points and grabbing 15 rebounds, but again getting little help from his teammates, only one of whom scored in double figures. Game four was more of the same, as Shaquille had 38 points, and Eddie Jones was the only other Laker to have more than three field goals. The score was 96 to 92. The sweep was painful enough for Shaq without having it pointed out that four of the six playoff series losses for his teams (Magic and Lakers) had been sweeps.

Again the year ended much too early for Shaq, but he had lots of plans for the summer. He would visit his parents in Orlando and his daughter in Houston, see lots of movies, and would be back for a couple of classes at LSU. In addition he planned to finish another rap CD and would take an intensive one-week course in film directing. He would also work out as hard as ever in the hope that 1998–1999 would be the season that he and the Lakers were able to win an NBA title.

PREPARING FOR THE 1998–1999 SEASON

One dark cloud hanging over the next year was a labor dispute between the NBA owners and the NBA players. Although there were many issues, they basically all came down to money—money for pensions, salary cap money, and endorsement money. The owners threatened to lock the players out of NBA practice facilities in the off season, and some players, like Michael Jordan, urged players to boycott the World Championships in Athens in July. Many did. Shaq had already declined, although he did not mention the labor dispute. He cited his busy schedule and his desire to continue course work at LSU.

During the early part of the summer, Shaquille was praised for donating five multimedia computers to a Los Angeles-area YMCA that had had a number stolen. Shaq read about the theft and swiftly offered his assistance. This was in keeping with a number of characteristics of O'Neal— well-informed, generous, concerned with poor youngsters, and savvy about publicity.

The NBA lockout began on July 1, the date that the old agreement expired. The hope was that the season would be able to begin on time, but many people were skeptical. Shaq was busy with a number of projects. One was creating his own brand of basketball shoe. The Reebok agreement had expired and the company chose not to renew it. Many shoe companies were following that lead in regard to high-paying endorsement contracts, dropping star players because they felt that they weren't worth the large payments by the companies. Shaq still had big endorsement contracts with Pepsi and Taco Bell and was developing a series of fairy tales for Scholastic publishers. Smaller deals with Kenner, Warner Brothers, A&M Records, and All Star Cafes were also in place. The A&M deal was a marketing and distribution agreement linking A&M and Shaq's TWIsM Record label. A new album by Shaq, "Respect," was scheduled for a September 15 release. Shaq shelved his studies in film directing that summer when he got the opportunity to direct a new comedy series for kids, "Cousin Skeeter," that would air on Nickelodeon in the fall. Shaq was very serious about his directorial ambitions, but he also recognized that his NBA career made all the other incomes and activities possible. So the lockout was of great concern to him, despite his many endorsements and sources of income. The new album was completed in September, but the NBA lockout was still no closer to a settlement.

At the end of October, the NBA Players Union declared that they were sticking together in their dissatisfaction with the owners' proposal for a new contract. At a five-hour meeting in Las Vegas, more than 240 NBA players, including Shaq, Michael Jordan, Charles Barkley, David Robinson, and Patrick Ewing, all spoke for union solidarity to help the young players, as well as the players who came before them who were unable to have the advantage of such excellent benefits when they played. A week later, Shaq sent personal letters to each of his Laker teammates urging them to stay in shape, to work out together, if possible, and stay together as a team in the lockout. He also offered to rent the gym at Southwestern College in Los Angeles for them to work out, if they were willing, because the players could not use the Lakers' facilities until the lockout ended.

The month of November was lost to the lockout and December was also looking lost when the NBA announced the cancellation of the 1999 all-star Game, scheduled to be played in February. In efforts to both stay in shape through game competition and to win public favor, a number of charity games were held in late December featuring NBA players. One was in Atlantic City featuring Patrick Ewing, Karl Malone, Penny Hardaway, Alonzo Mourning, and Reggie Miller. Another game was played at UCLA and featured Shaq, Eddie Jones, Chris Mills, Elden Campbell, and WNBA players, Tina Thompson and Lisa Leslie. Proceeds were to go to the United Way, the Hollenbeck Foundation, and the Chris Mills Youth Foundation.

By Christmas, with the lockout/strike still not settled, NBA Commissioner David Stern set a date of January 7 as a deadline for settlement, after which the season would be cancelled. On January 6, one day before the deadline, both sides agreed to a settlement, with both giving a bit. The season would begin on February 2 and run for 50 games with full playoffs to follow. The training camps would be held for about two weeks before exhibition games began. The schedules for the year would be revised and announced later. "Later" was January 22. The season would officially begin February 5 and the Lakers would be the most televised team. Michael Jordan had retired for the second and final time so the Lakers, with Shaq and Kobe, became the new "media darlings." Nevertheless, most analysts were not picking the Lakers for the Western Conference crown. The Rockets, Spurs, and Jazz were all being favored over the Lakers, which upset Shaq. He predicted that he'd dominate centers such as David Robinson and Tim Duncan of San Antonio.

The season began with the Lakers taking three of their first four games, defeating the Spurs, but losing to the Jazz, once again. Shaquille averaged just over 30 points and 12 rebounds. Shaq missed game five of the season (a Lakers' loss) with a slight abdominal muscle pull, and there were fears that he'd repeat the injury problems of the previous year. But that did not occur and Shaquille didn't miss another game. The Lakers, however, didn't play very well and were just at .500 (six and six) when owner Jerry Buss fired Coach Del Harris. In addition the Lakers signed 37-year-old Dennis Rodman, one of the most controversial players to ever play in the NBA, but one of the best rebounders.

With a new coach, former Assistant Coach, Kurt Rambis, and the new power forward, the Lakers began playing better. They won nine games in a row to allow Rambis to tie the best start for a new NBA coach in history. When they did lose, to Sacramento, it was without Rodman, who was granted an indefinite leave for personal reasons. He ended up playing just 23 games for the Lakers. General Manager Jerry West then traded Eddie Jones and Elden Campbell to the Charlotte Hornets for Glen Rice, B. J. Armstrong and J. R. Reid. There was renewed talk of the Lakers strengthening themselves and making a title run. But, instead, the Lakers won only four of their next nine games to be 20 and 12 at the end of March, second in the Pacific to Portland. By mid-April they were 25 and 15, five games behind Portland with 10 games left. Coach Rambis was "singing the same song" that Del Harris had despite all the changes in personnel. He said that the Lakers needed to hustle more and cited only Shaquille as being consistently aggressive in each game.

In late April, Shaquille revealed something many had long suspected, that he and Kobe Bryant had "issues." The differences had been simmering for more than a year. Initially Shaq had tried to mentor Kobe since he entered the league right out of high school and Shaquille was the acknowledged star of the team, but the efforts had been more and more ignored by Kobe as he decided to go his own way, both on and off the court. Shaq expressed open frustration with the way Kobe was playing; Kobe expressed bewilderment, saying that he was trying to play good team basketball. What seemed to be needed was a forceful coach pushing them together for the benefit of the team. Neither Del Harris nor Kurt Rambis seemed capable of doing that. Shaq felt that Rambis and owner Jerry Buss were coddling Kobe and it was hurting the team. These problems would continue beyond the season.

The Lakers' stumbling end of the season finally stopped in the last game of April. Playing Portland, whom they had lost to twice in the year, the last time by 27, the Lakers responded with a resounding victory. The score was 108 to 89, with Shaq getting 38 points and 12 rebounds, including 14 of 17 free throws. The Lakers ended up winning their last four in a row to be 31 and 19, the Number 4 seed, and would face the Number 5 seed, Houston, in the first round of the playoffs. Shaquille finished second to Allen Iverson in scoring for the league. Shaq averaged 26.3 points and 10.7 rebounds, and led the league in field goal percentage.

THE 1999 PLAYOFFS

The Lakers opened at home against the Houston Rockets and edged them in the opening game, 101 to 100. Shaquille blocked a lay-up attempt with one second left in the game to ensure the Lakers' victory in a see-saw contest. Glen Rice had 29 and Shaq 27 points for the Lakers, and Shaquille also grabbed 11 rebounds. In game two, the Lakers came out fast, leading 31 to 12 after one quarter and coasting to a 110 to 98 victory. Shaquille not only had 28 points a game high, but seven assists, also a game high. Heading to Houston with a 2–0 lead, the Lakers appeared to have the series wrapped up.

The Rockets played their best game and defeated the Lakers 102 to 88 in game three as Shaquille made just nine of 22 shots for 26 points, still a team high. No one else had more than 13 points and Shaq also had 10 rebounds. It looked like Houston might come back, but Shaquille made sure that wouldn't happen after being critiqued by his father after Shaq's relatively poor shooting in game three. In game four Shaq shot 14 of 22 from the field and scored 37 points to go with 11 rebounds in the 98–88 Laker win. For the series, Shaquille averaged 29.5 points and 10.2 rebounds and was simply too quick and powerful for the Rockets and their veterans, Hakeem Olajuwon (age 36), Charles Barkley (36), and Scottie Pippen (34). It was a "changing of the guard" and the veterans noted it after the end of the series. Olajuwon said that Shaq was simply too strong and powerful and, even when Hakeem knew what Shaq was going to do, Hakeem could not stop him.

The Lakers would now play the San Antonio Spurs with Tim Duncan and David Robinson. The Spurs had finished the season in a tie with Utah for the best record in the league at 37 and 13, and the Lakers would have to work hard to make a series of this. They did not, as San Antonio swept the Lakers, the fifth elimination sweep in Shaq's career. He was getting tired of seasons ending in that manner. Game one was close, but went to the Spurs, 87 to 81. Shaquille was frustrated by having no fewer than four different players guard, grab, and foul him, limiting his touches and his points. He finished with 21 on 6 of 19 shooting, and after the game Shaq chased a referee off the court in an effort to confront him about the constant holding that he had endured. Coach Kurt Rambis prevented Shaq from getting to the referee, but the league fined Shaq anyway, for "not leaving the court in a timely manner." It cost him $7,500.

Game two was heartbreaking for the Lakers who led by one point with 19 seconds left and Kobe Bryant at the free throw line. He missed both shots, the Spurs scored, and got the ball back and hit two free throws. The final score was 79 to 76, with Shaquille leading L.A. in scoring with 16, but going 2 for 10 from the line. Game three in Los Angeles was close during the entire game and L.A. led, 91 to 90. Then the Spurs held the Lakers scoreless over the final 1:55 and scored 13 points to defeat L.A., 103 to 91. Shaquille had 22 points and 15 rebounds, but failed to score in the last 4:30. Game four was exciting. The Lakers were down the entire game and late in the third quarter were behind, 86 to 72. Then they scored 12 points in a row to close within 2 points, only to fade in the fourth quarter to lose 118 to 107. Shaquille had 36 points and 14 rebounds, but the Lakers' season was over.

NOTE

1. Shaquille O'Neal, *Shaq Talks Back* (New York: St. Martin's Press, 2001), 68.

Chapter 10

THE NEW LAKERS WITH
A NEW LEADER

In June 1999, the Lakers' owner, Dr. Jerry Buss, hired another new coach to replace Kurt Rambis. This coach was different, both because of the way he did things and because of his record as a head coach in the NBA. He was Phil Jackson, a 53-year-old native of Montana who had played for a number of years as a 6'10" backup center/forward on the New York Knicks, including two championship teams in 1969 and 1973. After assistant and head coaching jobs throughout professional basketball, he took over the Chicago Bulls in 1989. Jackson led the Michael Jordan teams to six NBA titles before resigning after the 1998 season. Jackson was tired of the general manager in Chicago and was "burned out," and he stayed out of basketball for a year before being pursued and hired by Dr. Buss. Jackson was not intimidated by players and he was very imposing, but at the same time he treated each player like the individual that he was. He practiced Buddhism and selected individual books that he thought players would benefit from reading. He also had the respect of the players because he had won six NBA championships.

Despite his great success, there was a general feeling that the Lakers would need a lot of help to be contenders for the NBA title in 1999–2000. A writer for the *Atlanta Journal-Constitution* was typical of this skepticism noting, "big-name coaches don't travel well. What worked for them in one place doesn't in another."[1] This writer felt that Jackson would need the kind of players that he'd had in Chicago to win an NBA title in Los Angeles, and it didn't seem that the Lakers had such players.

Most of the Lakers were excited about playing for Jackson. Leonard Armato, Shaq's agent, said that Shaq was excited about the Lakers' prospects for the future. That being the case, Shaquille decided to stay with the Lakers, rather than exercise the option in his contract that would have made him a free agent, able to sign with any team. Over the summer, besides increasing the intensity of his workouts, Shaquille, once again, returned for one term to LSU. He was closing in on his degree and was likely to complete his studies in order to get his B.S. degree in Business in 2000.

Shaq also visited Phil Jackson at his summer home in Montana. There he met Jackson's family and got to talk with him in a relaxed setting. Shaq was impressed and felt confident that Jackson was going to guide the Lakers to an NBA championship.

By September, when he reported to training camp, Shaquille felt that he was in the best shape of his career. He now weighed around 330 pounds on his 7'1" frame. The week before camp officially opened, Shaq went to a voluntary practice run by new coach Jackson and participated in several full-court games. Both Jackson and Shaq were pleased, and they were even more pleased when the Lakers announced that they had signed two veteran centers to back up Shaquille. With the addition of Benoit Benjamin and John Salley, it was hoped that Shaquille would get more rest time during the season, making him stronger for the playoffs. Shaquille commented on how much alike Phil Jackson and Shaq's dad, Phil Harrison, were. Besides the first name, they also disciplined in the same way and praised in a similar fashion. Shaquille said that he would work hard not to let either Phil down.

Lakers' General Manager, Jerry West, watched a lot of the early Lakers' practices and was greatly impressed by Shaquille's shape, mobility, and attitude. He predicted that Shaquille would be the most valuable player in the league in 1999–2000. Shaq was pleased and flattered by West's comments, but deflected the praise, saying that as long as the team did well, he was happy. He also said that he wanted to improve his defense this year, and he would be helped in that and his rebounding by the Lakers' acquisition of A. C. Green. Green had been a Laker from 1985 to 1993 and had won NBA championships. The hope was that he would add stability and experience to the Lakers.

The Pacific Division was seen by most writers as very deep, with the Lakers, Portland Trailblazers, and Phoenix Suns as legitimate contenders for the division and NBA titles. The Lakers had not won a division title since Shaq's arrival and most observers felt that there was not enough team strength on the roster to do so this year, but Coach Jackson's capability might provide for a better showing. The Lakers moved to a new arena, the Staples Center, and there were also indications that the differences between Shaq and Kobe Bryant had been resolved and they would be supporting each other, and the team, in their efforts to win an NBA title. Magic Johnson, the former Lakers' star and now a part owner of the team, offered the same prediction as Jerry West, that Shaquille would be the MVP of the league in 1999–2000.

Shaquille stated that he was very happy and observers agreed. Shaq often wore his emotions on his sleeve so "what you saw was what you got." He had matured in his personal life. He had a new girlfriend, Shaunie Nelson, and this relationship seemed stable and had the potential for longevity. They had one child together and Shaunie had one from a previous relationship. Shaq also had a son from an earlier relationship, so he now saw himself as the father of three and felt the need to stay home at night, rather than going out "clubbing," as he used to do. He was also surrounded and supported by his closest friends and confidantes, most of whom were friends from Newark, San Antonio, or LSU. An uncle and another acquaintance of his father's from Newark provided security and paternal advice on a daily basis, and Shaq still talked with both Lucille and Phil in San Antonio almost every day. Shaq had improved his eating habits after hiring a full-time chef, Thomas Gosney, who was also one of his closest confidantes. Gosney persuaded Shaq to stop bingeing on fast food and to eat healthier foods. Gosney also was available at any hour to make a meal for Shaq, so that he didn't even have to consider going out to eat in the middle of the night.

With Shaq and the team in a good frame of mind, the Lakers began the year hot and kept it up. Shaquille missed only two games all year, the second year in a row that he'd been able to stay injury-free, after two years of physical ailments. The exhibition season did not go as well as the Lakers would have hoped, as they had only three wins in eight games, and Kobe Bryant suffered a broken hand that would keep him out until December. Nevertheless, Coach Jackson was not totally displeased, as he got to see how various bench players fit into his offense. The regular season was a much different story from the exhibition games, as the Lakers won five of their first six games. Shaquille was playing very well, except for his free throws, and teams started using the "Hack-a-Shaq" defense even more. He was frustrated at both those tactics and his inability to make his free throws, as he was shooting only 35 percent. Shaquille lashed out at times and drew technical fouls and, against Houston, he and Charles Barkley engaged in a fight, which led to their ejections and subsequent suspensions for the next game.

Shaquille returned from his suspension, vowing to improve his free-throw shooting and keep his temper under control, playing a smarter game. He led the team to a 93–88 win over Atlanta, and the Lakers were an unexpectedly good six and two for the year. Shaquille was playing tremendously well, leading the league in scoring and field goal percentage and was near the top in rebounds and blocked shots. Against the Bulls in late November, he sank 19 of 31 free throws, while scoring 41 points, and he averaged 37 points a game over the last five games of the month.

By December 1, the Lakers had a record of 11 wins and 4 losses, but were tied with Seattle for third in the Pacific Division behind Sacramento (10–2) and Portland (13–3). The season was still young and the good start, even with Kobe Bryant sitting out, seemed to bode well for the remainder of the season. Shaq was playing hard and his enthusiasm seemed to finally be rubbing off, on a consistent basis, on the rest of the team. Phil Jackson had made a coaching reputation as a tactician and motivator, both of which suited Shaquille very well.

In December 1999, Shaquille and the Lakers really took off, winning 13 of 14 games in the month and opening a two-game lead on Portland in the Pacific Division. The team was buoyed by the return of Kobe Bryant in the first week of December, but it was Shaquille who was powering the Lakers to victory. Against the Golden State Warriors, he had 21 points and 13 rebounds in the first half, finishing with 28 and 23 in a 93 to 75 Lakers' win. Jerry West repeated his statement of the preseason, that Shaq was going to be the MVP of the league, calling his play "phenomenal" and saying that if Shaq wasn't the MVP of the league so far, the award didn't mean much.

On December 8, the Lakers' seven-game winning streak was broken in a 103 to 91 loss in Sacramento. Shaquille and Kobe each got 27 points, but Shaq was in foul trouble and had five turnovers while Kobe had six turnovers. It would be the Lakers' only loss of the month. The day after the Sacramento loss, Shaquille announced that he would not play for the Olympic team in 2000 in Sydney. He stated that he greatly appreciated the opportunity to play on two prior Olympic teams, but he thought that the U.S. team had enough strength, and he wanted to give other players a chance to play on the team.

Shaquille had the Lakers tied for the best record in the league by mid-December, and he was voted the NBA Player of the Month for November while averaging 28 points and 14 rebounds a game. He was still struggling with his free throws, shooting a career-worst 42 percent, but was also third in the league with 3.29 blocks a game, a career-high. The Lakers, however, were concerned that Shaq was playing about 40 minutes a game. They didn't want him worn down by the time the playoffs began, so they continued to seek a suitable backup. The players signed in the off-season had not worked out and the hope was that the Lakers could find someone within the next month.

Shaquille and Kobe Bryant were combining to be the best 1–2 punch in the league, with Shaq averaging 26.6 and Kobe 22.5 points a game since his return. Glen Rice was averaging 17.5 points in a supporting role, so the Lakers had lots of weapons to counteract defenses collapsing on Shaquille. Shaq had been ejected from a game for getting two technical fouls and had been subsequently suspended for one game, but he now was controlling himself better. The result was a more relaxed Shaq, better play, and more Lakers' victories. Even with playing more than 40 minutes a game, Shaquille felt that he was pacing himself and not wearing down.

In late December the first votes for the all-star game came in, and the voters seemed to agree with Jerry West. Shaquille led all Western Conference players in votes for the game to be held February 13 in Oakland, California. Right after that announcement the Lakers played the defending champion San Antonio Spurs in a very meaningful contest. Led by Shaquille's 32 points and 11 rebounds, the Lakers won by a score of 99 to 93. The victory also gave them the NBA's best record at 23 and 5 and thrilled a sellout crowd of nearly 19,000 at the Staples Center in L.A.

The Lakers started out 2000 the same way that they ended 1999. They reeled off six more victories to extend their winning streak to 16. In addition, Shaquille was getting more notice for the way he was leading the Lakers to all those victories. Players, coaches, scouts, and writers agreed that Shaq was the most valuable player in the league so far. In mid-January he continued to be a leader in four categories: second in scoring (27.8 points per game), first in rebounding (14.5 per game), second in field-goal percentage (57.6%), and third in blocks (3.18 per game). These statistics were even more impressive when it was noted that the Lakers were blowing out teams and Shaq often sat out the last six or seven minutes of games.

On January 14, the Lakers finally lost, 111 to 102, to the Pacers in Indianapolis. It was the Lakers' first loss since December 6 in Sacramento. Shaq blamed himself for the loss, as he only went 10 for 25 from the field in getting 22 points, but Jackson was not too upset, telling his team to get ready for Minnesota (their next opponent). The loss, however, seemed to upset the Lakers more than it should have, and they dropped four of five games to fall to a record of 34 and 10 at the end of January. Some teams thought that the Lakers were vulnerable and ready to fade as they had in other years. It wouldn't happen.

All-star balloting was announced at the end of January, and both Shaquille and Kobe were named starters for the West team. Shaquille was the leading vote-getter among the Western players, and Vince Carter was the overall leader by about 100,000 of almost 4 million votes cast by the fans.

The Lakers regained their focus as February began. They headed into the mid-February All-Star break with a three-game winning streak and a record of 37 and 11, a half-game behind Portland for both the Pacific Division lead and the best record in the league.

The all-star game resulted in a 137 to 126 West victory, its first in three years, and was keyed by the play of Tim Duncan and Shaquille. Shaq had 22 points, 9 rebounds, and 3 blocks in just 25 minutes of play; Duncan had 24 points and 14 rebounds, and they shared the MVP award for the game. Shaq felt both vindicated by finally receiving an award that he felt he had deserved in other games, and also a bit envious of Duncan, as he already had won an NBA championship. Shaquille was pointing to that as the highlight of the season, not the all-star game. Shaquille had been doing his part. At mid-season he still ranked in the top 10 of four of the eight major statistical categories.

On February 15, the Lakers went to Chicago, where Phil Jackson was soundly cheered by Bulls' fans, and beat the Bulls, 88 to 76. Shaquille scored 29 points, but made 11 of 12 free throws. For three weeks in February he was hitting nearly 70 percent from the line, and he credited his success to adherence to a new routine at the line. Near the end of the month, USA Today analyzed 10 top players' performances in 10 categories and declared Shaquille the NBA MVP, based on those data. Second was Kevin Garnett of Minnesota and third was Tim Duncan of San Antonio. Again Shaq was very pleased, but he did not want to lose track of his goal, an NBA championship. In that pursuit, the Lakers finished February with 11 straight victories and had the best record in the league, at 45 and 11, as March began.

The Lakers edged the Portland Trail Blazers, 90 to 87, on the first of March, extending their winning streak to 12 and moving past Portland for the divisional lead and the best record in the NBA. The Laker win also halted Portland's winning streak at 11 and the Blazers' home win streak at 16. A week later, the Lakers extended their win streak to 16, equaling their streak of earlier in the season, by beating the Clippers, 123 to 103. Playing on his 28th birthday, Shaquille scored 61 points, a career-high, on 24 of 35 shooting from the floor and 13 of 22 free throws. The crowd chanted "MVP" as Shaq went to the free-throw line late in the game.

The home crowds in L.A. were not alone in their thinking. As the season wound down and the Lakers continued to cruise to the best record in the NBA, more and more writers "climbed aboard the Shaq for MVP bandwagon." These same writers provided their reasons for his being MVP. He was no longer just a one-dimensional dunking machine, although he was virtually tied with Allen Iverson for the NBA scoring title. He now played great defense. His shot-blocking was ferocious. He was ready and able to toss the ball off for assists when double or triple teamed. He was making his free throws. (He finished the year with a .524 percentage, a big improvement for him.)

On March 14, the Lakers extended their streak to 19 straight wins in a 118–108 victory over the Denver Nuggets. Shaq had 40 points, despite playing with a sore hamstring, which he hurt a few days before. Two nights later the Lakers finally lost, in Washington to the last-place Wizards, 109 to 102. Shaquille had 40 points, but the Lakers' team defense failed them as they allowed Washington to hit 50 percent from the field. Despite the win streak ending, the Lakers remained resolute and they immediately went on another streak, winning the rest of their games in March and extending their lead over Portland to five games. Shaquille had had a fantastic month and was recognized as NBA player of the month for March, the same award that he had won in November.

The Lakers took this next win streak to 11 before losing to San Antonio on April 8. Shaq missed that game and the next one because of a severely sprained ankle, but on April 13, he returned to practice and then played against Sacramento on the April 14. By this time, the Lakers had a large lead over Portland and hoped to simply stay healthy and sharp for the playoffs as the season entered its final week.

The Lakers ended the season with an overtime loss, 103–98, to San Antonio. Shaq had 22 points, clinching his second NBA scoring title, and the Lakers finished with a record of 67 and 15. Their winning record and Shaq's overall performance for the year would likely bring him the MVP award, but Shaq and the Lakers wanted to go all the way in the playoffs and were keeping focused on that goal.

THE 2000 PLAYOFFS

As the Number 1 seed, the Lakers met the Kings, the Number 8 seed, in the first round. The Lakers, especially Shaq and Kobe Bryant, had destroyed the Kings in their four regular season meetings. Shaq had averaged 35.3 points per game and Kobe, 30.5, but the Kings had often hurt the Lakers in transition play, forcing L.A. into a lot of turnovers. Nevertheless, the Lakers were heavily favored to win the series and move on towards the NBA championship round.

The first game went as expected as Shaquille tied a playoff career high with 46 points as the Lakers won by a score of 117 to 107. Game two was even easier. The Kings double teamed Shaq most of the game, and he passed to teammates for easy scores. Shaq still ended up with 23 points, 9 rebounds, and 6 assists. The margin, this time, was 113 to 89, and there was talk of a three-game sweep. The Kings weren't quite ready to be swept.

Game three saw the Kings rally in the fourth quarter to win 99 to 91 and send the series to a fourth game. Shaq had 21 points and 17 rebounds, but missed 14 of 22 shots and was only 5 of 14 from the free-throw line. The troubles for Shaq and the Lakers continued in game four as Shaq went 10 for 22 (fine for most players, but quite disappointing for him), as he scored 25 points and 16 rebounds. The Lakers did not shoot well as a team and would need to improve on that when they returned to the Staples Center for the deciding game five.

Living up to his potential MVP award, Shaquille dominated the Kings in game five by scoring 32 points and taking down 18 rebounds in an easy 113 to 86 Lakers' victory. He out-rebounded the entire Kings' team in the first half. Afterwards Shaq said, "We never had a doubt we would play like that. This was a good test for us."

By finally defeating Sacramento, the Lakers set themselves up to play the Phoenix Suns, victors in four games over the injury-riddled San Antonio Spurs. Phoenix was the Number 4 seed in the West.

Phoenix was led by Jason Kidd, a point guard with incredible court vision and the ability to find the open man, and Penny Hardaway, Shaquille's teammate in Orlando. The Suns did not have a big man able to contain Shaquille, but in the first game of the series, the Suns played O'Neal with single coverage and Shaq destroyed that strategy. He scored 37 points, took 14 rebounds, and blocked 4 shots, as the Lakers hardly extended themselves in the 105 to 77 victory. The Suns' defensive strategy was ridiculed after game one, and game two saw O'Neal draw lots of double teams. It was not enough, however, as Shaquille played all but one minute of the game and scored 38 points and grabbed 19 rebounds as the Lakers escaped with a 97 to 96 win.

Just before the game, Shaquille was presented with the MVP trophy for the season by NBA Commissioner David Stern. The vote had been announced the day before, and Shaquille had received 120 of the 121 votes cast to get 99.2 percent of the votes cast. Shaq had finished the year leading the league in scoring with 29.7 points per game, as well as in field goal percentage with 57.4 percent. He was second in rebounding with 13.6 a game and third in blocks with 3.03. He also finished with a career-high 3.8 assists per game. The only controversy was why he didn't get all the first place votes (one went to Allen Iverson), and many columnists wrote about their perplexity in having a voter feel Iverson deserved the MVP more than Shaquille. Shaq laughed off the issue, but was clearly proud of his accomplishment. He said that he called his parents immediately and that his dad started crying. To Shaquille, this was all about the love and support that he had always received from Lucille and Phil. After the announcement, Shaquille chose to quote Aristotle, the ancient Greek philosopher, who said, "excellence is not a singular act, but a habit." Shaq said that he now wanted to be known as "the Big Aristotle." It was an interesting request, but it never caught on among the writers.

In Phoenix on May 12, the Suns tried to derail the Lakers and their MVP, but Shaq wasn't about to let his team down. Once again, he was dominant, scoring 37 points and snaring 17 rebounds to propel the Lakers to a 105 to 99 victory. Two nights later, the Suns managed to slow down the Laker express with a 117 to 98 win. Jason Kidd had a triple double, leading four Suns with at least 16 points. The Lakers got down early and never caught up. Shaquille, forced to sit for long stretches because of foul trouble, ended up with 24 points and 9 rebounds. The teams would return to L.A. for game five.

In what turned out to be the final game of the series, the Lakers displayed great defensive intensity, holding Phoenix to 65 points in an 87 to 65 victory. The Lakers did not shoot very well, but they held the Suns to 29 percent shooting for the game and 23 points in the first half. Shaq led the Lakers on defense by clogging the lane and on offense with 15 points. He also took 21 rebounds, one short of his career playoff high. As soon as the game ended, there was speculation about the next series against Portland, who had defeated the Utah Jazz in five games.

The Blazers had a big center (Arvydas Sabonis) who could shoot from the outside and, thus, draw Shaq away from the basket. They also had two strong forwards in Brian Grant and Rasheed Wallace who could take advantage of the smaller Lakers' forwards by posting them up down low. There was concern that the Blazers' strengths were the Lakers' weaknesses. The series would demonstrate whether this was true.

Game one was in Los Angeles and the Lakers burst out to a 21-point halftime lead. The Blazers crept to within nine in the fourth quarter and started fouling Shaquille, hoping that he'd miss free throws and allow them to close the margin even more. Shaquille foiled the strategy by hitting seven straight free throws, and the Lakers pulled away to a 109 to 94 win. Shaq had 41 points, 11 rebounds, and 7 assists. He also set NBA playoff records for most free throws attempted in a half (27) and a quarter (25 in the fourth). He finished 13 of 27 from the line. After the game, Shaq said that the "Hack-a-Shaq" strategy would not work. "You can't mess with my mind," he declared.

Game two, however, was a different story, as the Blazers slowed the game and the Lakers went ice-cold from the field. Portland embarrassed the Lakers by a 106 to 77 score, and a number of people started taking about a Blazers' victory in the series. Shaq had only nine points in three quarters, as the Blazers collapsed on him with double and triple teams. The Lakers scored only eight points in the third quarter to essentially put the game out of reach. Shaq scored 23 points in this game.. The pressure now shifted to the Lakers as the two teams traveled to Portland for the next two contests.

The Lakers regained their home court advantage by defeating Portland, 93 to 91, on a shot by Ron Harper with 29 seconds left. Shaq led the squad with 26 points and 12 rebounds and played all 48 minutes.

During commercial breaks in the series, television viewers also saw Shaq as he promoted a number of Internet and Web-based commercial services that provided, among other things, online audio and video to the site, immediately after Lakers' games. Shaq was not getting an endorsement fee, but, rather, stock options for this work. This practice is no longer unusual, but it was in 2000, and it reflected Shaq's interest in technology and his interest in having his own companies, rather than just endorsing for others. Shaq and his agent, Leonard Armato, began Dunk. net to sell athletic shoes and apparel of Shaq's endorsed design, which buyers could customize on-line. Shaq also advertised FreeInternet.com by wearing caps with the company logo, and he received a percentage of revenues generated by the Web site.

Game four saw the Lakers win their second in a row on the road in Portland, 103 to 91, giving L.A. a three-games-to-one advantage over Portland. Shaquille led the team with 25 points and 11 rebounds. Shaquille went nine of nine from the free-throw line, with six straight in less than two minutes in the fourth quarter as the Blazers tried the "Hack-a-Shaq" once again, but the strategy backfired. After the game, Shaquille said that his three-year-old daughter, Taahirah, offered the right coaching touch for him. "She doesn't really know the game," said Shaq, but she said, "Good luck and bend your knees." Shaq responded with his perfect free-throw shooting.

The Lakers seemed to have the series wrapped up as the teams returned to L.A. for game five, but things didn't go as they had hoped. Rather than running their offense through O'Neal, the Lakers shot 27 three-pointers, but converted on only 6, as the Blazers triumphed, 96 to 88. Shaquille still managed to get 31 points, but noted that the team blew its chance to move on by hoisting jumpers when he was easily available. Shaq said that they had "to play smarter" and Coach Jackson agreed. It didn't seem to have taken effect, though, in game six in Portland, where the Blazers defeated the Lakers, 103 to 93. Shaq took only 17 shots and hit 7, while going 3 of 10 from the free-throw line. Kobe Bryant had 33 points, but 12 came on three-pointers after the Blazers had a 13-point lead with less than five minutes in the game.

So Shaquille and the Lakers faced another elimination game, after seeming to have the series well in hand. Back in Los Angeles, the Blazers seemed to have momentum and opened up a 15-point lead on the Lakers in the fourth quarter. But then the Lakers, relying on their bench players, Robert Horry, Brian Shaw, and Ron Harper, mounted a comeback as the Lakers outscored Portland 31 to 13 in the fourth quarter. Shaquille had two free throws and a dunk on a lob pass from Kobe Bryant to finally give the Lakers a lead of 85 to 79 with 41 seconds left. L.A. finally triumphed, 89 to 84; Kobe scored 25 points and Shaq 18 points to lead the team. It was a draining victory and the biggest game seven fourth-quarter come-back in NBA history.

The victory set up a finals series with the Indiana Pacers, led by Reggie Miller, Rik Smits, and Mark Jackson. Indiana had finished 56 and 26, the top team in the East, then had knocked off the Milwaukee Bucks, the Philadelphia 76ers, and the New York Knicks to reach the finals. The series would open in L.A. on June 7.

The series started with a big game from Shaquille, and he kept it up throughout the series. In game one he scored 43 points and got 19 rebounds in an easy 104 to 87 victory for L.A. In game two the Pacers tried the Hack-a-Shaq technique, and it resulted in Shaq going to the free-throw line 39 times (an NBA finals record) in a nearly three-hour contest. He made only 18 free throws, but that combined with his 11 baskets for 40 points and 24 rebounds led to a 111 to 104 victory for the Lakers. All of the fouling stopped the flow of the game, dragged out the contest, lost television viewers, and subjected the Pacers and their Hall of Fame coach, Larry Bird, to criticism. Bird said that he hated the strategy, but he was trying to win a game, and this seemed to be the best option that he had. In the second quarter, Kobe Bryant sprained his ankle severely and even more of the Lakers' offense fell on Shaquille's shoulders. He responded well, but he still made the game close by missing the 21 free throws.

Despite the missed free throws, writers were now comparing Shaq with the all-time great centers, Wilt Chamberlain, Bill Russell, Kareem Abdul-Jabbar, and George Mikan, all of whom won at least two NBA championships (Chamberlain and Mikan had also won championships with the Lakers). With Shaquille and the Lakers on the verge of their first title, it seemed that Shaquille would finally achieve all that had been predicted for him. It was noted that Shaq was still only 28, and Michael Jordan and his Bulls had not won a championship until Michael was 28, so maybe

Shaq's years of "struggle" weren't so unusual. There were two more games to win, however.

With Bryant out of game three in Indianapolis, Shaq had little help in scoring or rebounding. He had 33 points, the next highest Laker scorer had 10. Shaq had 13 rebounds; no other Laker had more than 7. Indiana won the contest, 100 to 91. Bryant returned for game four and he led the Lakers to an overtime victory, 120 to 118, after Shaq had fouled out with 2:33 left in overtime. Even with Kobe's heroics and 28 points, Shaq was still the leading scorer with 36 points and 21 rebounds. For the series, Shaq was averaging 38 points and 19 rebounds per game, and the Lakers were just one victory from a championship. Game five in Indianapolis's Conseco Field House went to the Pacers as the Lakers' successful shooting abandoned them. Bryant shot 4 of 20 from the floor and the Lakers' bench players were almost as bad, going 6 for 23. Shaquille was the only bright spot for L.A., with 35 points and 11 rebounds. The two teams would return to California to end the series.

With the championship finally in sight, Shaquille scored 41 points and had 12 rebounds in leading the Lakers to a 116 to 111 victory and the NBA championship. He was named the MVP of the finals and became the third player ever to win MVP honors in the regular season, the all-star Game, and the finals in the same year. He was also one of only five players ever to score at least 30 points in every game of the finals. Shaq cried on the court as he hugged teammates and his family members, noting that he had always wanted this while growing up. It was, at the time, the highlight of his great career.

NOTE

1. Steve Hummer, "Don't Expect Jackson to Work Any Miracles in L.A.," *Atlanta Journal-Constitution*, June 18, 1999, E6.

Chapter 11

THE CHAMPION
LOOKS FORWARD

Shaq was on top of the world. The Lakers were NBA champions and he was the most valuable player in the league and the playoff finals. He was playing for a coach, Phil Jackson, whom he admired and who knew how to get the most from his players. Shaq's celebrated feud with Kobe Bryant seemed to be in the past. In his autobiography, *Shaq Talks Back*, published in 2001, Shaq noted that when he scored 61 points on his birthday, he and Kobe had bonded, and there were no other problems on the court after that. Shaq had a girlfriend, Shaunie Nelson, whom he was crazy about. He and Shaunie had a new son, Shareef, born on January 11, who was now six months old. His two houses in Orlando and Los Angeles were spacious, and his closest friends either lived with him or minded the other home when he wasn't there. His parents were healthy and comfortable in their new home in San Antonio. Shaq had furnished his homes with recording studios for his rap work, video games, and movie theaters to view his extensive collection of films. Everything seemed to be going right for Shaquille and he knew it. He was a happy man.

Shaq had begun some new marketing notions in conjunction with his agent, Leonard Armato, that had Shaq working as an independent company, rather than just for people as an ad "pitchman." Unfortunately, this was the beginning of the "dot.com collapse," a time in which many of the new, Internet start-up companies began failing as the economy worsened. Companies like Freeinternet.com went into bankruptcy, and Shaq lost close to one-half million dollars. Ultimately this would also lead to other Internet failures, including other efforts that Shaq had heavily invested in. This would be just one factor leading to Shaquille and Leonard Armato parting ways in 2002.

After the dream season, Shaq was in high demand on talk shows and for magazine interviews. He took a couple weeks of that before taking time off and treating his "team"—bodyguards, managers, chef Thomas Gosney, and some cousins to a few days in Las Vegas. He paid for about $10,000 of chips for each of them, and they camped in some expensive suites for a week. Shaq also paid $42,000 for a police car that had been destroyed in rioting in L.A. after the Lakers' win as fans "celebrated." Shaq's accountant had opposed this expense because he had nothing to do with the rioting, but it was something that Shaq wanted to do and it had a positive impact on his public relations.

In August Shaquille took his friends hunting at a game preserve in Florida. Shaq had gotten interested in hunting and frequented some of these preserves in the South and Southwest. He also was continuing to pursue another interest, police work. Shaquille was a volunteer deputy with the L.A. county police and was training to be an auxiliary member of the Port of Los Angeles Police and went on some police ride-alongs. His goal was to eventually work in law enforcement, and he continued to pursue that interest over the next few years. His uncle and others in his "entourage" were former police officers, so this interest was not surprising.

Over the summer of 2000, Shaq did more work for his degree at LSU. He was now down to a few credits, two courses in agriculture and geography, that would come from independent study courses that could be completed away from campus. His intention was to receive his degree on December 15, 2000 at the graduation ceremonies in Baton Rouge. Were he to be successful in acquiring his degree, Shaq would become eligible for the LSU Hall of Fame, as well as being able to have his number retired.

In October Shaq and Lakers' owner, Jerry Buss, agreed on an $88.4 million three-year contract extension. In celebration Shaq spent $150,000 on 22 Rolex watches for each of his teammates and Lakers' support staff. Shaq was a generous person who enjoyed giving gifts, and his teammates were swift to praise his generosity.

The Lakers management, particularly General Manager, Mitch Kupchak, was active over the summer. It had acquired a veteran power forward to strengthen the team and make another run at a title possible. In a series of trades and signings involving four teams, the Lakers acquired Horace Grant and Greg Foster, two big men, as well as some veteran guards, including Isaiah Rider, who might make the team. They had also drafted Mark Madsen, a big, strong forward from Stanford. The Lakers had traded Glen Rice and dropped A. C. Green. The team had the potential to be better in 2000–2001.

The Lakers were favored by many to win the Pacific Division and the Western Conference, as well as the NBA championship, but being favored only meant that teams would get up for playing the reigning NBA champions even more than ever. Indeed there were a number of observers who thought that Portland had strengthened themselves enough to win the Pacific Division and, maybe, the NBA championship. There was no disagreement over the fact that the Western Conference was far superior to the East. The Blazers, the Lakers, the San Antonio Spurs, the Phoenix Suns, the Utah Jazz, the Dallas Mavericks, and the Sacramento Kings were all seen as superior to almost any team in the East. Getting out of the Western Conference playoffs and into the finals was predicted to be more difficult than winning the NBA finals. That was nearly nine months in the future; the season had to be played first!

The Lakers began the season playing well, but not as well as the previous season, mostly because of the tough competition in the West. By the end of December, the Lakers were 18 and 9, but Sacramento was 17 and 7 for a half-game lead.

In mid-December, Shaquille, with the support of the Lakers, missed a game against the Vancouver Grizzlies to attend graduation ceremonies in Baton Rouge, Louisiana, at LSU. It had taken him eight years, but he had fulfilled the promise made to his parents to get his degree. At the graduation ceremonies, Shaq drew laughter and applause, when he spoke to his classmates and declared that he felt very secure now that he had a degree to fall back on and could get a real job. That evening he saw his LSU jersey number 33 retired and raised to the rafters just before the LSU-New Orleans basketball game. Shaq then flew to Toronto to join the Lakers for a game against the Raptors.

On January 26, Shaquille sustained a foot injury, later diagnosed as a strained arch, in a game and was forced out of the lineup until February 13, after the all-star game. Shaq had been voted to the starting lineup, once again, but was unable to play. Shaquille was frustrated by both the injury and the inability of the Lakers to play together as much as they had the year before. Kobe and Isaiah Rider were shooting more without working the ball around, and there were other injuries to players like Derek Fisher, who was out until March and played only 20 games during the regular season. Shaq had told Lakers' General Manager Mitch Kupchak that he wanted to be traded a month before, but neither Kupchak nor Leonard Armato acted on this request, figuring Shaq was just expressing his frustration.

When Shaq returned to play, the Lakers were third in the Pacific Division, with a record of 32 and 17. Sacramento was a half-game ahead and Portland was at 37 and 15, 3 1/2 games ahead of L.A. Allen Iverson was leading the league in scoring with 30.3 points per game, and Kobe

Bryant was second at 29.9. Shaquille was sixth in the league with his 27.0 average.

By the end of the month, the Lakers had closed to within a game of Portland, and at the end of March they were still one game back, but to Sacramento; Portland had slipped to third. At that time Derek Fisher came back as the Lakers' point guard, and Isaiah Rider was dropped from the team. Bryant was out with shoulder, then ankle, problems, but Shaquille had returned to lead the Lakers with his enthusiasm and play. He had upped his scoring to 28.1 points per game, fourth in the league, just behind Kobe's 28.7. He had upped his rebounding to more than 12 per game and was third in the league, as well as first in field goal percentage.

The Lakers closed the season by winning their last eight games in a row, edging the Kings by one game for the Pacific Division title and securing the Number 2 seed in the West behind San Antonio, who had finished two games ahead of the Lakers with a record of 58 and 24. Shaquille had been superb down the stretch and won the NBA player of the month award for April. He had averaged 33.7 points per game to increase his season average to 28.7, third in the league. He also finished the season by hitting 13 straight free throws and hit 66.5 percent of his free throws over his last 17 games. Both he and the Lakers were peaking at the right time.

As the playoffs opened Shaq's newest autobiography, *Shaq Talks Back*, was released to generally favorable reviews. Shaq comes across as very human, humble in many cases, confident in others. The text is interspersed with copies of letters from relatives and friends who offer their views of various events and times in Shaq's life. The book covers up to the aftermath of the first World Championship for the Lakers and Shaq.

The first round of the playoffs had L.A. facing Portland, who had stumbled to the finish, ending up fourth in the Pacific and the Number 7 seed in the West. The Lakers swept the Blazers in three games, with the closest a seven-point victory. Shaquille led the Lakers in game one with 24 points, despite hitting only 7 of 21 shots, but 10 of 15 free throws. Game two saw Shaquille dominate with 32 points and 12 rebounds, as the Lakers won by 18 points, 106 to 88. The series ended with a 99 to 86 Lakers' win. Shaq had 25 points and 15 rebounds.

The swift defeat sent the Lakers into a second round match-up with the Kings, who they had edged for the Pacific title and who nearly defeated them in the playoffs the year before. The Lakers continued their dominant play, sweeping Sacramento with the closest game being a three-point opening game, 108 to 105. In that game, Shaq scored 44 points and had 21 rebounds. Lucille attended the game and Shaq made frequent eye contact with his mother who sat directly across from the Laker bench.

In game two Shaq's dad, Phil Harrison, was in attendance and Shaq had 43 points and 20 rebounds. He became the first player in NBA history to have back-to-back 40 point, 20 rebound games. The score was 96 to 90.

In game three the Kings double-teamed Shaq consistently and held him to 21 points, but Kobe and the rest of the Lakers scored easily in the 103 to 81 rout. The same pattern continued in game four, as Shaq had 25 points and 16 rebounds and Kobe scored a career-playoff high of 48 as the Lakers swept again, 119 to 113. The Lakers had now won 15 games in a row and had not lost in six weeks.

The announcement of League MVP was made at this time, and the award went to Allen Iverson who had led the league in scoring and steals while leading his team to a 56 and 26 record, the best in the East. Shaquille finished second.

The Conference finals would pit the Lakers against San Antonio, the team with the best record in the league and two big superstars, Tim Duncan and David Robinson. But the Lakers rolled over San Antonio in four straight games, with only one being somewhat close. In this series Shaq struggled a bit because of the difficult Spurs' big men, but he was still outstanding. In game one Kobe Bryant scored 45 points, and Shaq had 28 points and 11 rebounds in the 104 to 90 win. Shaq downplayed his problems with Kobe, declaring that he told Kobe that he (Kobe) was Shaq's idol; he later told reporters that Kobe was the best player in the game when he plays like he did in the win. Phil Jackson commented positively about their newfound camaraderie and their teamwork. Their understanding of each other's strengths in exploiting the weaknesses of the other team was breathtaking, and the results were fabulous.

In San Antonio, the Lakers' dominance continued, although game two was only an 88 to 81 win. Shaq had 19 points with 14 rebounds and Kobe had 28. The victories were some revenge for the Spurs' sweep of the Lakers in 1999, the last time that the two teams had met in the playoffs. The Lakers were looking to return the favor.

In L.A., Shaq scored 35 points and had 11 rebounds in a Lakers' rout, 111 to 72. Kobe scored 36 points and 8 assists, and the end of the series seemed already decided. Game four was a formality, as Shaq had 26 points and 10 rebounds and even led a full court fast break in the lead guard position as L.A. won, 111 to 82 to propel the Lakers into the NBA finals with 11 straight playoff wins, 19 total, and two months without a loss.

The Lakers would meet the Philadelphia 76ers in the finals. Led by Allen Iverson, the 76ers had defeated Indiana, then edged both Toronto and Milwaukee in seven close games. The Lakers were heavily favored, but in game one in L.A., the 76ers surprised L.A. with a 107 to 101 overtime victory. Shaq had a fantastic game, with 44 points and 20 rebounds, but he didn't get the usual support from Kobe Bryant and the rest of the Lakers. Shaq hurt the cause by missing 12 of 22 free throws. Allen Iverson scored 48 points, including 7 in overtime.

The second game was a Laker victory, but the big story was Shaquille's near quadruple-double. He had 28 points, 20 rebounds, 9 assists, and a finals-record-tying 8 blocks. The score was 98 to 89. Games three through five would be in Philadelphia. In Philadelphia Shaq and his friends were given a special tour of the Philadelphia Zoo, the nation's oldest. It turned out that Shaq was quite enamored of zoos and animals, having visited zoos throughout Asia, Australia, and Europe when giving clinics. He had also visited zoos in almost all NBA cities, although it was tough for him to appear in such public places without setting off "mini-riots" and impromptu autograph sessions.

The Lakers edged the 76ers in game three, 96 to 91. Shaq sat on the bench for much of the game because of foul problems, mostly as a result of Dikembe Mutombo's "flopping" when Shaquille turned into him on offense. Still, Shaq had 30 points and 12 rebounds and managed to play 41 minutes. In game four Shaq scored 34 points and had 14 rebounds as the Lakers won their third in a row, 100 to 86.

The Lakers' ultimate victory in the series seemed to be conceded by many writers, and they began praising Shaquille as one of the all-time great centers because of his championship play. In four games he had averaged 34.5 points and 16.5 rebounds and was only one assist behind Kobe Bryant. Kobe said that Shaq was "the most dominant player in the world" and few would argue that point. Shaq's adept passing had surprised the 76ers and had set up many baskets for L.A. in the series.

Game five was not close and the Lakers and Shaq repeated as NBA champions. Shaquille scored 29 points and took 13 rebounds and was supported by Kobe Bryant's 26 points and 10 rebounds; the Lakers won, 108 to 96. The season had ended with 23 wins in 24 games, and the Lakers' record of 15 wins in 16 game in the playoffs gave them the best winning percentage in one year, as well as a record for most consecutive playoff road victories. Shaquille averaged 30.4 points per game in the 16 games, as well as 15.4 rebounds. In the finals, he was even better with averages of 33 points and 15.8 rebounds, and he was named MVP of the finals for the second consecutive year.

It had been a great year, once again, for Shaq, with another championship, another NBA finals MVP award, and, finally, the awarding of his college degree from LSU. Shaq would find almost as much accomplishment, however, in the next season.

IN SEARCH OF A THIRD CHAMPIONSHIP
IN 2001–2002

During the off-season, Shaquille spent some time in Orlando at his home there, hunted, made some commercials, and spent a lot more time with Shaunie Nelson and their children in Los Angeles. At the end of the summer, Shaquille had surgery on the little toe of his left foot to correct a claw toe deformity. He would be unable to run for six weeks, and there were doubts about his ability to play for the Lakers' season opener. Even if he were to play, he would not be in shape and he would be playing himself into shape, playing as much as he would able to handle. This did not bode well for the Lakers, and some questioned why he hadn't had the surgery earlier in the summer.

Despite concerns that his recovery might be slower, Shaq was in training camp in mid-October, just a bit late and still slowed by not having run for six weeks. He worked hard and was in the lineup for the opening game of the season against Portland. Shaq and Kobe Bryant each had 29 points as the Lakers won by 12. Shaq also had 18 rebounds, 5 assists, and 5 blocks. Although not fully recovered, Shaq jump started the Lakers to a record of 19 and 3 by the end of December, the best record in the league, but only a half-game better than San Antonio's 19 and 4 record. The Lakers had added a new power forward in Samaki Walker and had the starting lineup from the previous year intact; they were favored to win the NBA title once again.

After their hot start, the Lakers had some problems. Shaq missed three games after being suspended for swinging at an opponent in a game. He also continued to have minor problems with his feet, which sometimes limited his playing time. The Lakers didn't play together as well as they had at the end of the prior championship year, and there were renewed rumors of Kobe and Shaq fighting over the way Kobe did (or didn't) distribute the ball. By the beginning of February the Lakers had fallen behind the Sacramento Kings by three games. Dallas led the Midwest Division with the second best record in the league behind the Kings. Shaq and Kobe were third and fourth in league scoring, both around 26 points per game. Both were also voted to the starting line up of the all-star game, which was held in Philadelphia on February 10.

Shaq was having problems with his toe, once again, and was forced to miss the game. He also remained out of the lineup for the next couple of weeks. Shaq's absence stimulated a number of articles lamenting the shortage of true centers in the NBA and saying that he was really the only dominant one now playing. His injury kept him out of the lineup, hurting both the Lakers and attendance at Lakers' games. Shaquille tried a lot of cures including prescription pain killers, physical therapy, electronic stimulation, and various foot creams; but the pain, exacerbated by arthritis, was finally too much and he was on the injured list until February 19, when he returned to score 25 points and grab 17 rebounds in a victory over the Celtics.

Shaq continued to play well, but his minutes were limited to allow him to rest and not aggravate his toe. Shortly after Shaq's return, Bryant was suspended for fighting and missed a couple of games, but Shaq led the team to victory in those contests. He even wore Kobe's jersey in warm-ups as a tribute to Kobe. Despite their on-again, off-again disagreements, both recognized that they had to play together to provide the Lakers with a third straight NBA championship. One of the games Kobe missed was on March 5, the day before Shaq's birthday, when he always had a big game. This year was no exception (although, technically, it wasn't on his birthday since the Lakers had an off-day on March 6). Shaq scored 40 points and had 12 rebounds, as the Lakers defeated the New Jersey Nets, the top team in the Eastern Conference, 101 to 92. He also made only 8 of 20 free throws. Before the game Shaq was given a birthday cake with purple and gold icing (the Laker colors) and three candles, one for each decade. The win put the Lakers' record, 42 and 18, one game behind Sacramento. Catching them was a good goal because of the desire to keep home court advantage during the playoffs, but keeping Shaq healthy was most important.

From mid-March the Lakers went 15 and 6, but fell three games short of the Kings for both second in the Pacific Division and second in the NBA overall. Shaq ended up playing in 67 (of 82) games and was second in the league in scoring (27.2 points per game) and first in field goal percentage, once again, while getting 10.7 rebounds per game, the eighth best average in the league and tied for his lowest rebound average in his career. He was feeling better, despite having to soak his toe in ice after each game and taking anti-inflammatory pills.

THE 2002 PLAYOFFS

The Lakers would open the playoffs against Portland, who had faded badly in the second half of the season and finished nine games behind L.A. to become the Number 6 seed. The first two games were reminiscent of the previous year's playoffs, as the Lakers had two wins, with Shaq and Kobe leading the way. In game one Shaq scored 25 and Kobe scored 34 points in a 95 to 87 win. Game two was similar, as Shaq scored 31 and Kobe scored 19 points in the 103 to 96 victory. Shaq also had 14 rebounds to lead all players in that category. Game three in Portland was much tougher and required a three-point basket by Robert Horry with 2.1 seconds to go in order for the Lakers to edge the Blazers, 92 to 91, and capture the series in three straight games. Shaq had 21 points and 11 rebounds and hit 11 of 16 free throws. Bryant had 25 points, and both he and Shaq played 45 of 48 minutes. Shaq was tired and his toe hurt a bit after the game, but he was glad to end the series quickly and send the Lakers on to the Conference semifinals against the San Antonio Spurs, who had finished the season with the same record as the Lakers, but had struggled in their first round series, edging Seattle in five games.

There was great anticipation for this series because Tim Duncan and David Robinson would both be healthy, and the Spurs would be looking to avenge the Lakers' sweep of the year before in the Conference finals. The series began in L.A. and the Lakers won game one, 86 to 80, with Shaq scoring 23 points and getting 17 rebounds, despite slicing open his right index finger in the third quarter, requiring him to receive three stitches, which forced him to miss 10 minutes of the contest. That morning he had gotten cut on some glass while playing with his kids and needed four stitches in his left wrist. Shaq would be nagged by various injuries and pains for the rest of the series.

Both Shaq and Kobe Bryant (who had left game one with a bruised knee) were held out of practice, but returned for game two. The Lakers went down by 21 points in the first half, but rallied at the end to close the gap, but still lost, 88 to 85. Shaquille had just 19 points and 7 rebounds, struggling to grasp the ball with his stitches still intact. The series would shift to San Antonio, with the Spurs displaying new confidence.

In between games two and three, the NBA announced that Tim Duncan of the Spurs had edged Jason Kidd of the Nets for MVP of the season, with Shaq a distant third, although he had played in only 67 games. The awarding of the MVP to Duncan, it was thought, might motivate Shaquille a bit more to play better against the best. In game three, before more than 35,000 people in the Alamodome, however, Shaq seemed to still be limited by his injuries, as he scored only 22 points, but grabbed 15 rebounds. In addition to his stitches, he was playing on a sprained left ankle and favoring his arthritic right big toe. Kobe Bryant took the lead for the Lakers with 31 points.

Game four was tight, and the Lakers won, 87 to 85, on a shot by Kobe Bryant. Shaq had 22 points, 11 rebounds, and 5 assists, but was displeased by his play and hoped that more treatment for his toe and ankles would help in game five.

The Lakers were up three games to one and wanted to end the series swiftly to have more time to heal. They were successful, defeating the Spurs, 93 to 87, as Kobe had 26 points and 8 rebounds, and Shaq had 21 points and 11 rebounds. The Lakers would have three days off before opening the Western Conference finals in Sacramento against the Kings. They would need a healthier Shaquille to win this series. Sacramento had stopped the Utah Jazz in four games, then defeated Dallas by a four-games-to-one margin. They had finished three games ahead of the Lakers in the standings and wanted to prove that their finish as the best team in the league was no fluke.

The series opened in Sacramento before what was called the best home crowd in the league, but they couldn't inspire their favorites enough to beat the Lakers in game one. Shaquille (26) and Kobe Bryant (30) led the Lakers to a 106–99 victory. Two nights later (May 19), the Kings reversed the outcome, winning 96 to 90. Shaquille had 35 points, but Kobe Bryant, weakened by food poisoning, scored only 22 points in 40 minutes of action. Despite the loss, the Lakers felt that they would win once they returned to L.A. and Kobe regained his strength.

The Kings regained the home court advantage in game three by winning, 103 to 90. The Lakers kept shooting three-point shots, despite missing 13 of their first 16, and Shaquille hardly received the ball in the low post. He did finish with 20 points and 10 rebounds, but the Lakers continued to misfire throughout most of the game. In game four, Robert Horry again saved the Lakers' season with a three-pointer with less than a second remaining to give L.A. a 100 to 99 win. The Kings blew a 24-point lead to send the game back to Sacramento tied at two games each. Shaq scored 27 points and snared 18 rebounds to lead the Lakers, with support from Bryant's 25 points.

As the series paused for a travel day, it was noted that Shaquille and Hedo Turkoglu of the Kings had hugged and touched cheeks before the opening tip of each game. O'Neal explained that it was a Muslim form of respect. It may have been the first time that many fans had even realized that Shaq was a Muslim. Lucille, his mom, was a Christian, but his father, Phil, had converted to Islam as a young man. Shaquille had chosen to follow that faith.

Back in Sacramento, the Kings edged L.A. 92 to 91, putting the Lakers one game from elimination. Shaquille was in foul trouble much of the game and was able to play only 32 minutes, yet scored 28 points on 14 of 18 shots. He fouled out with just over three minutes to play and the Lakers down, 85 to 84. L.A. shot only 26 percent as a team, as no one but Shaquille seemed to be able to find the basket consistently. The Lakers would have to shoot better in game six, and Shaquille would need to get more free throws while fouling less or the Lakers' season would be over.

In game six, Shaq went 13 of 17 from the foul line, including 10 straight at one point, as part of a 41-point outburst that drove the Lakers to a 106 to 102 victory. He also had 17 rebounds and had support from Bryant's 31 points and 11 rebounds. The series now turned to a decisive seventh game in Sacramento on June 1 and, fittingly, the game went to overtime before L.A. won, 112 to 106. Shaquille, again, rose to the occasion by scoring 35 points, taking 13 rebounds, making 11 of 15 free throws and blocking 4 shots. Shaq noted, after the game, that they never gave up and that the focus that came from Coach Phil Jackson taught them how to be champions. But there was still another series to play to make that a reality once again. That would be against the Eastern Division Champions, the New Jersey Nets, led by Jason Kidd, who had topped Indiana, Charlotte, and Boston to enter the finals.

The series did not prove to be as close or entertaining as the Western finals, as the Lakers swept the Nets in four games. Jason Kidd played brilliantly, but Bryant and Shaq were too much for the Nets. Kobe scored 27 points per game, but Shaq was the dominant force once more. He scored 36 points per game, shooting nearly 60 percent from the floor. He also averaged 12 rebounds, 4 assists, and 3 blocks (all records for a four-game series) and was the MVP of the NBA finals for the third year in a row.

With the victory L.A. and Shaquille clearly established themselves as one of the greatest teams and players in NBA history. Great teams and players need to win championships to prove their greatness, and the Lakers and Shaq had done that. Shaq felt he had little left to prove to anyone.

After the Lakers' third consecutive NBA title, as well as Shaquille's third consecutive NBA finals MVP, a number of articles compared Shaq with the greatest centers in the history of the NBA such as George Mikan, Bill Russell, Wilt Chamberlain, and Kareem Abdul Jabbar. These comparisons all included Shaq as the newest member of the "greatest NBA centers club." Shaquille explained that he had focused more on winning championships over the past three years, rather than making movies, doing albums, or just having fun. But he had now achieved his goal of winning championships, and both he and the Lakers were intent on winning a fourth in a row the next year.

CAN SHAQ AND THE LAKERS WIN FOUR CHAMPIONSHIPS IN A ROW?

Shaq did have a new interest, law enforcement, that he pursued in the off-season with the idea of a career change after his playing days ended.

He trained with the Port of Los Angeles Police Department before being designated as a second-class reserve officer. This entitled him to ride as "second man" in a patrol car and to carry a gun. Over the next two years, Shaq continued his training in the off-season in Los Angeles, and he continued this training with the Miami Beach police after his trade to the Miami Heat in 2004. In December 2005, in a private ceremony, Shaquille was sworn in as a reserve police officer in Miami Beach. Shaq continues to work on patrols in the off-season (at a salary of $1 per year), but it seems unlikely that he will ever spend lengthy time on this "career." At one time he stated that he hoped to be a sheriff in Louisiana or Orlando, but he has not seriously pursued that goal.

During the entire off-season of 2002, Shaq's arthritic toe continued to bother him, and he visited numerous foot specialists seeking relief for the pain. In August, Shaq battled a virus, which caused swelling in his liver, and set back a decision to have surgery, once again, on his toe. The operation was finally performed at UCLA Medical Center in September, and the recovery period was estimated at eight weeks, meaning that Shaq would again miss training camp and the beginning of the season. The surgery involved removing bone spurs in the arthritic toe joint and was deemed successful, as his range of motion increased almost immediately. Shaq began rehabilitation in two weeks, hoping to return by the start of the season.

Much of the consulting about Shaq's surgery involved his business manager, Mike Parris, and his new agent, Perry Rogers (also tennis star Andre Agassi's agent). Shaq and Leonard Armato agreed to part company, and Shaquille and Rogers had reach an agreement during the spring of 2002. One unusual investment of Shaq's time and money was a decision to invest in a $100 million real estate deal that would provide low-income housing for people in Colorado. Shaq and Parris began investing in real estate in New Jersey in about 1998 and this continued Shaq's interest.

Shaquille began the season on the injured list, weighing 342 pounds, although he noted that his body fat was only 17 percent. On November 22, he returned to score 17 points in 21 minutes in an 86–73 victory over the Chicago Bulls. The Lakers had struggled without him and the win gave them only their fourth win in 13 games. A week later Shaq had 33 points and 11 rebounds in a victory, but the Lakers were still just 5 and 11. Both Shaq and Kobe Bryant were pushing their teammates to work harder and play better, but the Lakers were only 13–19 at the end of the year, despite Shaq shooting 57 percent from the field, the league leader in field goal percentage.

A big change in Shaq's life occurred on December 26 when he and Shaunie Nelson were married at the Beverly Hills Hotel. Their two children, Shareef and Amirah, ages 2 and 1 years, attended the wedding, and the Shaq and Shaunie were expecting a third child within a few months. Married life seemed to agree with him. Shaq's shooting was astounding in the games after he was married, going 24 of 33 (72.3%).

The Lakers battled back from the deep hole that they had dug for themselves, going 37 and 13 the rest of the regular season to finish 50–32, second in the Pacific and the fourth seed in the Western Conference. The Lakers topped Minnesota in six games to open the playoffs, then faced San Antonio in the conference semifinals. The teams split the first four games before San Antonio won the next two, the last a 110 to 82 blowout in the Staples Center. Playing on a sore knee, Shaquille had 31 points and 10 rebounds in the game, but the Lakers had no answer for Tim Duncan and the younger, quicker Spurs. The loss raised questions about how the Lakers would rebuild for the next season. Shaq expressed both his pain at losing and his hope to return to the championship the next year. After missing games, Shaq still managed to score 27.5 points per game, average 14.8 rebounds, and shoot .574 from the field (second in the league). In the playoffs, he had more than 30 points per game and more than 15 rebounds, but it was not enough. How strong could he be the next year at age 31?

THE LAST SEASON AS A LAKER

Mitch Kupchack, the General Manager of the Lakers, took action in the off-season to get the Lakers back on top of the league. He managed to sign both Gary Payton and Karl Malone, free agents and two future Hall of Fame players. They were both near the end of their careers and were willing to sign with the Lakers for less money than they could get elsewhere because they had never won a championship and felt that, with the Lakers, they could. Many media journalists were conceding the title to the Lakers, and Shaquille expressed his great pleasure at the addition of the rugged forward from the Utah Jazz (Malone) and the tough point guard from the Seattle Supersonics (Payton). Shaq was also pleased that David Robinson of the Spurs had retired, and all of these things made him seem confident that the Lakers would be back in the championship round the next spring.

Within a week, however, things started to turn sour for the Lakers. In late July Kobe Bryant was charged with sexual assault in Eagle County, Colorado, where he had been undergoing rehabilitation for his knee. The charges and the trial weighed on Bryant and the entire Laker team. Bryant managed to keep his focus while going through training camp and the beginning of the season, despite flying back and forth to Colorado for hearings.

The season started off well with Laker victories and the team playing together, but then, in late November, Shaquille suffered a strained calf muscle that plagued him for much of the year, reducing his mobility and jumping ability. Without Shaq the Lakers were a much weaker team and it showed. They won 18 of 21 games to open the season, then won only two of six games without Shaquille. Shaq returned and the Lakers played better, but then Malone went down with a hamstring injury. By the end of 2003, they were 20 and 7, but were playing inconsistently. Then Shaq reinjured his calf and was out again in early January. He returned in late January but had two sore calves, which hampered his play. Bryant's surgically repaired shoulder was limiting him at times and Malone was out for two months.

Despite all the injuries and inconsistent play, the Lakers were still second in the division by the beginning of February, with a 28 and 16 record, behind Sacramento's 33 and 12 mark. For the first time in a number of years, Shaq was not voted in as the starting center for the all-star game, losing out by 31,000 votes to Yao Ming of the Houston Rockets. The Lakers were playing without Malone and, often, without Kobe, who was in and out of the lineup with knee, finger, and shoulder ailments. His relationship with Coach Jackson was also becoming more strained, and the coach turned to Shaquille and Rick Fox, the two most veteran Lakers, for help in trying to improve the relationship and the team's "chemistry." The rift between Kobe and the team seemed to diminish, but the Lakers' management was displeased with remarks that Coach Jackson had made, that Shaq, not Kobe, was the focal point of the team. The team announced that they would put negotiations with Jackson over a new contract on hold. This seemed to mean that Kobe was the focal point of the team and that would certainly add to the strain under which the Lakers were operating.

The Lakers went 10 and 4 in February, and Shaquille scored 24 points in the all-star game to earn another MVP award, so the season seemed to be improving. In March the Lakers were 13 and 3, and on April 2, they were briefly the top team in the league at 53 and 23, a remarkable turnaround. Then Kobe stopped playing team ball once again, and the team closed with three wins in the last six games to end up 56 and 26 and the Number 2 seed in the West and the Pacific Division Champion. Despite missing15 games and limping through pain in a number of others, Shaquille still averaged 21.5 points and 11.5 rebounds per game for the season. He also led the league in field goal percentage, with 58.4 percent, and was eighth in the league in blocks, with 2.48 per game.

None of this would matter as the Lakers faced Houston in game one of the playoffs. The Lakers exhibited a strong team effort in defeating the Rockets, four games to one, and would now face the defending champions, the San Antonio Spurs. Shaq averaged 22.5 and Kobe 26 points per game to lead the Lakers to a four-games-to-two series victory. Shaq also grabbed 13.5 rebounds per game. The Lakers looked like they were heading to another title, now that they had eliminated the Spurs. Next up would be the Minnesota Timberwolves and MVP, Kevin Garnett.

The Lakers triumphed, again in six games, with Shaq averaging nearly 21 points and 16 rebounds per game. Kobe scored 24 points a game, but took twice as many shots as Shaq in the series. The offense was meant to run through Shaq more and, despite the victories, there was continued tension between Shaq and Kobe. The finals would pit the Lakers against the Detroit Pistons, who had upset the Indiana Pacers in six games. The Pistons emphasized strong team defense and an offense with no one star.

In an unexpectedly easy series, the Pistons topped the Lakers in five games. Shaquille scored nearly 27 points per game and Kobe 22 (although he shot only 38% from the field). The rest of the Lakers didn't provide much help, whereas all five Detroit starters averaged in double figures.

The end of the season was also the end of both Phil Jackson and Shaquille's careers as Lakers. Both were "discarded" in favor of keeping Kobe Bryant happy as the center of the Lakers. Jackson, in fact, returned to the Lakers as coach a year later. In July, 2004, Shaquille was traded from the Lakers, at his request, after Jackson's departure to the Miami Heat for three players and a draft choice.

Chapter 12

SHAQ JOINS
THE MIAMI HEAT

After eight seasons with the Lakers, Shaquille would return to Florida where he began his pro career, but about 250 miles south of Orlando, in Miami. He would retain his home in Los Angeles, where he was still active in the entertainment business and where his wife's parents still lived. Shaq wanted to let the Los Angeles fans know how much he appreciated their support over his years there, so he took out a full-page ad in the *Los Angeles Times* to express his thanks. The ad said, in quoting O'Neal, "I want to thank you from the bottom of my heart for your incredible support over the last eight years."[1] It included a photo and talked of his future and that he'd never forget the fan support in L.A.

Shaq also wanted to meet and greet the Miami fans. In late July he stood outside the American Airlines Arena in Miami and spoke to more than 3,000 fans, promising to bring a championship to Miami. He talked about his time with the Lakers, his admiration of new Coach Stan Van Gundy, teammates Dwayne Wade and Eddie Jones, and how good he felt physically. He joked a bit and thoroughly charmed the fans.

In the fall, Shaquille agreed to some in-depth interviews with various reporters, and these revealed that he felt that the Lakers had made him a scapegoat for their failures to win a championship the last two years. He also responded to concerns about his weight, saying that he was big-boned and that muscle was heavier than fat. He said he weighed 335 pounds. He also noted how much he was looking forward to returning to L.A. for a nationally televised game on Christmas Day. The game, however, would be less important than his passing out toys to 5,000 to 10,000 kids in L.A. as he had in the past, as "Shaq-a Claus".

THE 2004–2005 SEASON

The Heat's performance in most of the 2004–2005 season was as Shaquille and the Miami fans had hoped. The league had been realigned into six divisions, three in each conference, but there would still be only eight teams from each division in the playoffs. The Heat seemed assured of one of those slots. They had two young starters in Dwayne Wade and Udonis Haslem and two veteran starters in Eddie Jones and Chuck Person. Shaquille would be the dominant center that they had been missing. The only problem might be a thin bench, but that would not hurt them much during the season; but it would come back to haunt them in the playoffs. Miami was in the new Southeast Division and by the first of December they were in first place, with a modest record of 10 wins and 6 losses. The team was learning to play together and Shaquille was trying to be, as usual, a team leader. He had said from early on that this was "Dwayne Wade's team" and Wade's scoring did reflect that. He was sixth in the league in scoring at this early juncture with 25.2 points a game and Shaquille was averaging about 21. What was most heartening was that Shaquille felt strong and was not nagged by any injuries. In the much anticipated Christmas Day game, the Heat edged the Lakers in overtime, 104 to 102. Shaq had played Shaq-a Claus to 250 youngsters on Christmas Eve and played a solid game the next day with 24 points and 11 rebounds.

In January the team really began to gel and won 14 of 15 games that month to be solidly in first in both the division and the conference, with a record of 24 and 7. Both Phoenix and San Antonio had better records in the West, still considered stronger, overall, than the East. At the end of January Wade's scoring had dropped a bit to 23.7 points per game, and Shaq was at 21.5. The leader was Kobe Bryant with 28.4 and the Lakers' record was 15 and 12. Shaq was also Number 6 in rebounding, with 10.7 per game. Still, Shaq took himself to task because of his poor free-throw shooting, which was at 46 percent, a career low. He noted that he'd need to shoot much better at "playoff time."

All-star voting began in January and Shaq was the runaway leader for Eastern Conference Center. When voting stopped on February 3, Shaq had received the second highest vote total ever and would start at center in the game on February 20 in Denver. It was Shaq's 12th consecutive all-star game appearance. Shaq and the East squad would be coached by the Miami coach, Stan Van Gundy, because the Heat had the East's best record. In the game, itself, Shaq played very well, getting 12 points, 6 rebounds, 3 steals, and 3 blocked shots, and he entertained the crowd with dance moves and a cell phone in his shoe. Allen Iverson was MVP in the East's 125–115 victory.

The Heat went back to work and by the end of February had a record of 42 and16, by far the best in the Eastern Conference. Shaquille had also improved his performance, with 23.1 points (11th in the league) and he had maintained his rebounding average (10.5), which was fifth in the league. He had also remained injury free and played in 53 of the Heat's 55 games. With Shaquille and Dwayne Wade (23.5 points per game), the Heat were seen as the favorite in the East. At the end of the season, they had the best record in the Eastern Conference, 59–23, five games better than the defending champion Detroit Pistons. The Phoenix Suns had the best record in the West and the NBA with 62–20. San Antonio matched the Heat's record. Shaquille had finished with an average of 22.9 points, 10.4 rebounds, and 2.3 blocks per game. His field goal percentage of 60.1 percent was the highest of his career. He was named to the NBA first team for the year, and he seemed ready for a great playoff series.

Miami swept the New Jersey Nets in the opening series in four games. Then they swept the Washington Wizards in four games in the Eastern Conference finals. They would now face the Pistons for the Eastern Championship and, with Dwayne Wade and Shaq playing so well, the Heat were favored. The teams split the first two games, with Wade and Shaq leading the way, both with scoring more than 20 points a game, and Wade averaging 28 points for those games. In game five, the Heat opened a lead of 20 points when Wade was injured with five minutes to go in the third quarter. The Pistons sliced the lead to 10, but the Heat recovered to win by 12 points, 88 to 76, as Shaq led the team with 20 points. The Heat needed only one victory to move into the NBA finals, but Wade's injury, a pulled rib cage muscle, made that victory problematic. Earlier in the playoffs, Shaquille had sustained a deep thigh bruise and was not at 100 percent, but he was not going to stop playing.

Wade was unable to play in game six and the Pistons easily won, 91 to 66. Shaquille had 24 points, but the rest of the team labored badly. Game seven was in Miami and Wade played, although obviously in pain. He scored 20 points, but did not shoot well (35% from the field) and was weak at the end of the game when he was most needed. Shaq had 27 points, 9 rebounds, and 3 blocks, but it was not enough as the Pistons won, 88 to 82. Shaq was crushed by this defeat and shouldered much of the blame, despite his fine performance and Wade's injury. Shaq had promised Miami a championship and now, at 33, might be too much past his prime to deliver on his promise. Shaq wanted to renegotiate his contract, and he had to decide whether he wanted to return to Miami or some other team, or not play at all.

Despite the frenetic pace of the playoffs, Shaquille managed to show his great humanity, once again, when Hall of Fame Center, George Mikan, died during the Pistons' series. Mikan was 80 and was the first great big man in the NBA for the Lakers' franchise, then in Minneapolis, before the team moved to Los Angeles in 1960. Shaq had met Mikan, who had diabetes and kidney-related problems when he passed away. Shaq recognized Mikan's impact on the game as well as the financial problems that Mikan's ailments had created for his family. Thus Shaq offered to pay all of the Mikan family's funeral expenses as a tribute to George Mikan. Shaq said, "Without George Mikan (who was the biggest star of the game in the 1940s and 1950s), there is no me." Shaq's sense of history, his generosity, and humanity were legendary among his teammates and friends. These types of acts only made him seem even bigger than life.

SHAQ NEARS THE END OF HIS CAREER—WHAT NEXT?

During the early part of the summer of 2005, Shaquille and his agent, Perry Rogers, considered what he might do for the next year and beyond. He had a contract that paid him $30.6 million for the next year, but they asked the Miami Heat management to agree to end the contract and allow him to sign a new contract for $100 million for five years. The Heat agreed, as it both saved them money and meant that Shaq would remain a member of the team. The reason that Shaquille proposed this was to give the team more financial flexibility in signing free agents, thus improving the team and making a championship more possible. Shaq was interested in more championships, rather than more money, although he would still be the highest paid player in the league. With the money that the Heat were able to save, they acquired in trade Jason Williams and James Posey from the Memphis Grizzlies for Eddie Jones, and then signed Antoine Walker, a free agent of the Boston Celtics. Later, perennial All-Pro Gary Payton was also signed.

Also during the summer Shaquille completed an MBA degree from the University of Phoenix, an almost exclusively on-line university. In an effort to both market a new product and make it more accessible to all, Shaq created a new basketball shoe, which would retail for less than $40, available at a discount shoe chain.

Hurricane Katrina devastated the Gulf Coast on August 29, and Shaquille organized a drive for food, clothing, bedding, medical items, and major appliances soon afterwards. He and his family helped collect donations, and Shaq helped load 18-wheelers that left from south Florida loaded with the supplies. They also rented 400 apartments in the Dallas area to help house evacuees who had fled the storm.

Shortly after the beginning of the season, Shaquille suffered a severely sprained ankle that sidelined him until early December, by which time the Heat were 10 and 8. Then Coach Stan Van Gundy resigned to spend more time with his family, and Pat Riley, the President of the Heat, came back as the coach. From that point on, the coincidental returns of Shaq and Riley brought the Heat a record of 42–22 to finish the season as the Southeast Division champion and the Number 2 seed in the East.

In January, Shaq and Kobe Bryant had been publicly reconciled in Los Angeles, when O'Neal had approached Bryant before their game, congratulated him on the birth of his daughter, and the impending birth of his second child. They then hugged and seemed to put their differences behind them. Shaq credited the great Hall of Famer, Bill Russell, who told Shaq to initiate this settlement, and he did as ordered. Ironically, it had been announced in November that both Shaunie Nelson O'Neal and Vanessa Bryant were due to give birth in early May. Amazingly, each had her baby on the same day, May 1, Vanessa Bryant in Orange County, California, and Shaunie O'Neal in South Florida. The baby, Mearah Sanaa, was Shaquille's third daughter, joining Taahirah and Amirah. He also has three sons, Myles, Shareef, and Shaquir. Two of the children are from previous relationships, and he and Shaunie now had four children of their own.

In the first round of the playoffs, the Heat met the Chicago Bulls, the Number 7 seed, who had closed their season with a rush to edge into the playoffs. In the series the Heat struggled through four games, but pulled away to defeat the Bulls in games five and six to win the series. Shaquille dominated the decisive game six with 30 points and 20 rebounds in the 113–96 win. Shaquille became the second oldest player to get at least 30 points and 20 rebounds in a playoff game. With the victory, the Heat faced the New Jersey Nets in the Eastern Conference semifinals. Shaq and the Heat had an easy time defeating the Nets in five games, setting up another Detroit Pistons-Miami Heat Eastern Conference finals series. Shaq was playing better and feeling better than he had in two or three years. The Heat, led by Shaq and Dwayne Wade, burst out to a three games to one lead before knocking off the Pistons in six games. In the decisive game six, Shaquille was the Shaq of old, leading the Heat with 28 points and 16 rebounds. It was on to the NBA finals against the Dallas Mavericks.

The Mavericks seemed to be too deep and too fast for the Heat, as Dallas jumped out to a two games to none lead. Shaq's 2 of 16 free throw shooting in those games was a factor in the losses, too. But, then, in Miami, the Heat swept all three games, then defeated the Mavericks in game six in Dallas to win the NBA championship. Despite Shaq's weakest NBA finals ever (12.7 points per game and 9.7 rebounds per game), he had his fourth championship ring. His promise made to the fans of Miami more than two years before of a Miami championship had been fulfilled.

So, now, what's ahead for Shaquille, the most entertaining of NBA players? He has won championships, become a multimillionaire, and invested his money wisely enough to not worry about his financial future. He has also continued to be enormously generous with his time and his money, contributing to far more causes than he ever gets credit for doing. He does this because he is a genuinely nice person who never forgets what he did and didn't have as a youngster. He always had love and knows how important it is to everyone. He didn't have money, but recognizes that he can help so many people so he does. He has a loving wife and six great children. Playing with them he can remain a child a little longer. He likes to dress in costumes, to host parties, to take his friends hunting, and to sing and dance. His life is better than he ever imagined, but as good as he hoped it would be. He has provided for his parents and numerous friends and relatives. He has more cars than he can count and video games and old movies that he enjoys seeing over and over. Yet, he also gains great pleasure just from taking his children to the zoo, although that isn't as easy as it is for most people because of his instant recognition.

Will Shaq want to play again next year at the age of 35? He claims that he has never been happier and that he wants to stay and help the Heat win a championship, but he recognizes how much he has slowed down. Is it time to retire and become a deputy marshal? Or maybe just a wealthy businessman? He will certainly continue to invest in property that can be made available to those with low incomes, as he combines his business sense with his social responsibility. Or will he want to own or operate an NBA franchise like Joe Dumars, the president of the Pistons and former NBA All-Star; Magic Johnson, a partner in the Lakers; Michael Jordan, a partner in the Charlotte Bobcats; or Larry Bird, the Indiana Pacers president? Whatever choice he makes, Shaquille O'Neal will do it with enthusiasm or not at all. He is a literal giant among us and a man we'll not see the likes of again.

NOTE

1. "Lakers Fans Get Thanks From Shaq," *The Washington Post*, July 27, 2004, D2.

APPENDIX: CAREER RECORDS

Shaquille O'Neal Career Record
Position: C   **Height:** 7' 1"   **Weight:** 300 lbs.
Born: March 6, 1972, in Newark, NJ
College: Louisiana State University

Totals Year	Age	Team	League	Game	MP	FG	FGA	FT	FTA	TRB	AST	BLK	PF	PTS
1993	20	Orlando	NBA	81	3071	733	1304	427	721	1122	152	286	321	1893
1994	21	Orlando	NBA	81	3224	953	1591	471	850	1072	195	231	281	2377
1995	22	Orlando	NBA	79	2923	930	1594	455	854	901	214	192	258	2315
1996	23	Orlando	NBA	54	1946	592	1033	249	511	596	155	115	193	1434
1997	24	Los Angeles	NBA	51	1941	552	991	232	479	640	159	147	180	1336
1998	25	Los Angeles	NBA	60	2175	670	1147	359	681	681	142	144	193	1699
1999	26	Los Angeles	NBA	49	1705	510	885	269	498	525	114	82	155	1289
2000	27	Los Angeles	NBA	79	3163	956	1665	432	824	1078	299	239	255	2344
2001	28	Los Angeles	NBA	74	2924	813	1422	499	972	940	277	204	256	2125
2002	29	Los Angeles	NBA	67	2423	712	1229	398	717	715	200	137	199	1822
2003	30	Los Angeles	NBA	67	2535	695	1211	451	725	742	206	159	229	1841
2004	31	Los Angeles	NBA	67	2464	554	948	331	676	769	196	166	225	1439
2005	32	Miami	NBA	73	2492	658	1095	353	765	760	200	171	262	1669
2006	33	Miami	NBA	59	1805	480	800	221	471	541	113	104	230	1181
14 Seasons				941	34791	9808	16915	5147	9744	11082	2622	2377	3237	24764
82 Game Average					3032	855	1474	449	849	966	228	207	282	2158
Career High				81	3224	956	1665	499	972	1122	299	286	321	2377

Drafted by Orlando Magic in the 1st round of the 1992 NBA draft.

Per Game

MP/ game	FG/ game	FGA/ game	FT/ game	FTA/ game	DRB/ game	RE/ game	AST/ game	STL/ game	BKS/ game	TO/ game	PF/ game	PTS/ game
37.9	9.0	16.1	5.3	8.9	9.6	13.9	1.9	0.7	3.5	3.8	4.0	23.4
39.8	11.8	19.6	5.8	10.5	8.5	13.2	2.4	0.9	2.9	2.7	3.5	29.3
37.0	11.8	20.2	5.8	10.8	7.3	11.4	2.7	0.9	2.4	2.6	3.3	29.3
36.0	11.0	19.1	4.6	9.5	7.7	11.0	2.9	0.6	2.1	2.9	3.6	26.6
38.1	10.8	19.4	4.5	9.4	8.7	12.5	3.1	0.9	2.9	2.9	3.5	26.2
36.3	11.2	19.1	6.0	11.4	7.9	11.4	2.4	0.7	2.4	2.9	3.2	28.3
34.8	10.4	18.1	5.5	10.2	6.9	10.7	2.3	0.7	1.7	2.5	3.2	26.3
40.0	12.1	21.1	5.5	10.4	9.4	13.6	3.8	0.5	3.0	2.8	3.2	29.7
39.5	11.0	19.2	6.7	13.1	8.8	12.7	3.7	0.6	2.8	2.9	3.5	28.7
36.2	10.6	18.3	5.9	10.7	7.2	10.7	3.0	0.6	2.0	2.6	3.0	27.2
37.8	10.4	18.1	6.7	10.8	7.2	11.1	3.1	0.6	2.4	2.9	3.4	27.5
36.8	8.3	14.1	4.9	10.1	7.8	11.5	2.9	0.5	2.5	2.9	3.4	21.5
34.1	9.0	15.0	4.8	10.5	6.9	10.4	2.7	0.5	2.3	2.8	3.6	22.9
30.6	8.1	13.6	3.7	8.0	6.3	9.2	1.9	0.4	1.8	2.8	3.9	20.0
36.8	10.4	17.9	5.4	10.3	7.9	11.7	2.8	0.7	2.5	2.9	3.5	26.2